THE CUTTING

CRIME & TRAGEDY IN AN ERA OF PRISON OVERCROWDING

FOUR-PIECE

SCOTT THOMAS ANDERSON

Coalition for Investigative Journalism

For inquires about volume orders, please contact the book's distributor:
Small Press Distribution
Email: spd@spdbooks.org
Phone inquires: (510) 524-1668
Mail inquires:
Small Press Distribution
1341 Seventh Street
Berkeley, CA 94710-1409

The Coalition for Investigative Journalism is a club for professional and free-lance
reporters who are trying to preserve the critically wounded art of investigative journalism.
For more information, visit: cijournalism.com

The production of this book was made possible by advisory and logistical support from
Manzanita Writers Press, a nonprofit publishing house in California and private financial
donations by citizens using Kickstarter.com, a website for following and funding the Arts.
This book was written with the assistance of three professional journalistic editors and one
professional scientific editor. The book was produced with editorial coordination from the
Coalition for Investigative Journalism, a national club based in California.

Cover photograph of Angola Prison, in Louisiana, by photojournalist Chelsea Tucker.
All Rights Reserved.

To Stacy,
The only light I could have followed
to the end of this.

YEAR I

*"A Four-piece: A full set of restraints, composed
of handcuffs, leg irons and waist chain, and
security boxes to cover the restraints' key holes,"*

—The Atlantic *'The Ghetto Penthouse'* on prison lingo

*"There's a hole in daddy's arm
where all the money goes,"*

—John Prine Lyrics to *Sam Stone*

CHAPTER 1

February, Ione, California: News

MATTHEW LEARNED GLANCES up at Preston Castle, the prison's tower erect and its blood-ochre bricks redder than the rose shadow glazing the sky. He can see dusk fading from orange to porcelain over its abandoned arches, darkening the gothic turrets to match trees that run graywashed down the weedy headland. The larger slope under Preston bottoms into a creek crooking through Ione's downtown, and as Learned comes nearer, he glimpses white beaded lights trickling across the tops of little western storefronts.

Six years clean from methamphetamine, Learned tells himself, and three years out of the penitentiary: Welcome back to the town whose trailer park did it all.

A wraith of warm shit crackles in his sinuses. He worries he can still detect the feces of strangers emanating from his skin, an ordeal he confronted while battling ruptured sewage pipes in his apartment three hours before. He steps down Church Street. Ahead is a two-story café—an old, standing snapshot from when Victorian charm collided with breakneck life on the cattle lands: Tonight its centuried elegance is lit against the hills, its blue Art Deco marquee thrust up in the cold light of sundown.

People stroll through the café's doors. It is a lot of faces, and the ex-convict gradually begins to realize they've arrived to see him. Learned is about to speak at a meeting on methamphetamine and crime in the region. He's the only man taking the stage tonight that does not hail from the world of journalism or the ranks of law enforcement: Learned's invite comes by way of being a former meth cook and a recent guest at San Quentin and Pelican Bay prisons. He knows the audience will be watching him. And it is far more people than he ever expected.

Approaching the café, Learned spots two men in suits—a reporter he's become friends with and a man with a .40-caliber and gold star hooked to his belt.

"Thanks for coming," the reporter says. "I want to introduce you to Detective Josh Crabtree from the Calaveras County Sheriff's Department. He's one of the speakers tonight."

Learned shakes the cop's hand without hesitation, peering through a window of the café. "Lot of people," the ex-con observes, his mind flying back to the ruptured plumbing in his Sacramento apartment, sewage spilling through his sinks and showers, forcing him to spend the afternoon wrenching tools against an onslaught of filth. He could barely get clean before driving here. His jeans and T-shirt are loose. His head is cracked with exhaustion.

"Nervous?" Crabtree asks.

"A little," Learned mumbles.

"Well, not as nervous as me."

"Really?"

"Yeah, I've never spoken in front of a crowd like this before."

Learned tries to take solace in the words though he's haunted by the knowledge that his notes for the event are back at the apartment, abandoned victims of the fecal typhoon.

"Look," Crabtree adds, "no matter how worried you are about this, you've got to understand how much these people are going to appreciate you being here. And they're going to have a lot of questions, because, out of all the speakers tonight, you're the one who has the answers that they really want."

Answers, Learned thinks to himself. Answers to the rampant methamphetamine use that's still pushing crime waves throughout California while tearing its families to pieces? Answers about the overcrowded and buckling state prisons that have been on the front page of newspapers for months now? Answers about the bridge between the two, with rage as its deck and pain as its anchor span? Would they want to know what it's like to watch women pulled out of rundown apartments by their hair, the furious toggle-flex of their scalps rocking as their cheeks and chins are pummeled by a man's fists? Such is the kaleidoscope of addict-on-addict crime pirouetting the consciousness of those in the shadows. Learned remembers getting lured into an apartment and seeing a skinhead pull out a knife as his partner locked the door, grabbing Learned from behind with a hand around his mouth. That had happened in the supposedly quaint, peaceful county this event is taking place in tonight. Learned had bit those fingers across his mouth down to the bone, and then kicked the door through its deadbolt to escape before the skinhead could cut into him. Will the audience want to know that?

Prison, Learned thinks, the crowd will be asking about prison. He can borrow a phrase from old war veterans: "It's ninety percent sitting around being bored and ten percent being scared as hell." While Learned believes violence inside prisons is exaggerated by the media, the flashes of brutality he's witnessed are permanent contours of his brain shape. He came to understand quickly in Deuel Vocational Institute that disrespect, when it happens, is dealt with "there and then." It was in DVI Learned first saw an inmate get run through with a shank. Disrespect. In San Quentin, he witnessed a convict get pushed over the side of a tier, dropping four stories to the cement. The watermelon split of that man's cranium is still crisp in Learned's ears. Disrespect. On his first day in Pelican Bay, Learned glanced through a window to see an inmate get his throat cut by a rival holding a toothbrush lined with a razor blade. Learned would never know what caused that incident; but the prime suspect was disrespect. And beyond the rules of prison culture were more unpredictable threats. Working at correctional fire camp in Hemet, Learned and two inmates were charged by a schizophrenic prisoner who had gotten a hold of a butcher's knife in the kitchen. Screaming up to voices that circled his skullcap, the berserker lunged straight for the three convicts. He was slashing wide. One of the inmates managed to grab him. Learned and the other tackled him down. They heard the ranting. They pressed on the slow-motion insanity. All three inmates called for help. "There are cracks in the system," Learned says. "The guy with the butcher knife just slipped through one of them."

Is this what the crowd wants to know?

Learned slips into the café. He drifts anonymously through the huddled shoulders and warmth. A group at a nearby table discusses California's new law, AB 109, better known as Realignment. The legislation just went into effect. In the simplest terms Learned's heard it explained, Realignment combats California's massive problems with prison overcrowding by funneling thousands of freshly convicted inmates into county jails rather than state prisons. While murder, armed robbery and some types of felony assaults and sex crimes can still send a convict to a penitentiary, trafficking heroin, cooking methamphetamine and many property crimes no longer will: That's now a ticket for county jail, and in ninety-three percent of California's counties, those jails are already completely full with prisoners awaiting trial—men and women being held for committing real crime in real time. In some cases, the new "county prison inmates" are being sent home on ankle monitors or forms of alternative sentencing. The more Learned hears about the law, the harder it will be for him to wrap his mind around its import: If he was arrested for the same crime today that sent him to Pelican Bay for four years before, cooking methamphetamine, Realignment would now mandate he'd be shipped to county jail instead, where overcrowding would almost automatically send him home with an electronic ankle bracelet. Learned has also been told that all convictions for trafficking, selling and manufacturing narcotics, along with a number of crimes committed to feed addictions, will mostly mean "county prison terms," and, in reality, ankle bracelets.

Can a nylon strap and plastic box tame a full-tilt dope fiend? Can an ankle monitor steer those dependent on a substance like meth to stop stealing from family, robbing strangers, assaulting friends and letting children wallow in filth? Learned doesn't know if those are the questions he will be getting tonight. His best guess is that the inquiries will be about the nexus between addiction and criminal rehabilitation. But Learned never saw any rehabilitation, not in prison at least.

Learned looks up to see the journalist taking the stage. It will only be a matter of minutes now. Time to face them. Time to open up about staring into the predatory abyss—that existential vacuum of perjuries, control and bilateral abuse. Learned searches for a way to explain his view that cracking addiction and turning from crime is a personal decision. Telling a convict what he or she needs to do is an act of redundancy. They know what they need to do, he thinks. The instructions are condescending. Naive. Counter-productive. If the topic comes up tonight, Learned will say that asking an inmate what specific assistance he or she needs with education, employment or independent living are far more legitimate questions; though even those queries, in his mind, could only matter if the state's criminal justice system had a better intelligence for distinguishing sincerity from the manipulation that is as second nature as breathing to longtime addicts.

If only.

"Ladies and gentlemen," the reporter's voice says through the sound system, "I'd like to welcome Matt Learned."

Learned walks around the shoulder of the county sheriff, stepping onto the stage amid a loud, garbled smack of applause.

Watching at the back of the audience is Corporal Tom Oldham of the Calaveras County Sheriff's Department. Like Crabtree, Oldham lives in Amador County but works in the ranchlands across the river. The veteran deputy observes Learned speak to the attentive faces. He eventually exits the front of the café and heads home.

Three weeks pass for Oldham in a blur of routine patrols, and the meth awareness night in Ione lingers in his mind as part of a larger question of what Central Gold Country citizens know about the epidemic. Oldham has investigated an unending string of burglaries within his own beat that—when the suspect is caught—becomes a story circling back to meth addiction. But what is harder to forget is the emaciated senior citizens he's seen lying in beds, covered in open sores, while their addict children drain their bank accounts; or the babies he has found crawling through dog excrement on the floor of their addict-parents' meth houses. In his seven and a half years as a deputy, Oldham's been in more than a few high-stakes physical fights with men amped on a meth-fueled frenzy. More public awareness around what the drug can drive people to do, as far as Oldham is concerned, might help the public understand what deputies in Calaveras are up against.

On March 15, Oldham climbs into his cruiser at the sheriff's department in San Andreas. He begins his morning patrol by heading east on Highway 4 for Arnold. By 8:20 a.m. he's making a routine check on a bank alarm when, just miles up the mountainous roadway, a technician from Ebbetts Pass Gas Service has a jarring experience. It comes out of nowhere. Parking his truck along Blue Lake Springs Drive, the technician gets out and feels a man grab him from behind. He's suddenly looking at 44-year-old Kevin Duey, rattled and ranting. Duey has been awake for an unknown legion of hours. At 3:40 a.m., Duey phoned sheriff's dispatchers to report something like forest phantoms lurking in his yard. He added that they were "freaking him out." Now, the technician can't see the crystal meth pipe in Duey's sweatpants but he can see the loaded 9mm pistol in his hand. Unhinged, Duey holds onto the technician and waives the gun near his face. He blabbers about ephemeral assailants inside his house. It's a poltergeist of paranoia. And then Duey lets the worker go, running into the woods.

Ballistics evidence will later map out how Duey engages the specters. He charges through the trees, moving up a terrain lined with the omni-shadowed corners of vacation dwellings. He breaks into an opening on Dawyn Drive—a spot where a group of children had been waiting for a school bus ten minutes before. To Duey's immediate right is a chocolate T-frame house with a massive fern growing through its front porch. Duey looks over to the property's woodpile, firing a round into the front headlight of a Dodge Ram pickup. He then moves up the driveway of 664 Dawyn Drive. He passes a crumbled wound in the hill where massive pine roots are knuckling out of red dirt. Approaching a cottage, Duey fires a shot, drilling a bullet deep into the bottom railing of its front porch. He then runs up, grabs onto a storm drain and begins trying to scale up the side of the house. Hanging from the pipe, he fires another shot down into the wood of the front porch.

Sheriff's dispatchers reach Oldham at the bank. Only a few units of information chirp between the frequency's buzz-hum. The main knowledge Oldham has is that a gas technician is calling in a possible armed residential burglary. The deputy starts speeding toward Blue Lake Springs Drive. En route, the radio stays alive with new reports of homeowners hearing shots fired. Calls to 911 over gunfire are not uncommon on the edge of the Stanislaus National Forest; but as Oldham takes the descent down Moran Road and pulls up next to the technician's gas truck, he knows the bullets aren't flying from hunters: The deputy rolls his window down to see the tech, white-faced, urging and repeating, "Don't let him kill you, man! Don't let him kill you!"

Oldham now tunes his thoughts into the pistol fire echoing around the trees. He starts to follow the shots in his patrol car. The discharges whack louder through the timberline. Oldham stops his cruiser along a wooded embankment on Moran Road. He climbs out with his AR-15 rifle. The deputy approaches the opening of Dawyn Drive, a steep canyon-like path splitting an eclipse of ponderosa pines with early daylight. He breaks up a berm swept in coiling gold pine needles. A bullet slams through the branches. It's resonate—a percussive brass-rip jumped with a fading whomp-cough. Years of pulling targets on Marine Corps firing ranges have given Oldham an ear for proximity. He knows the round snapped the air just over his head. Duey comes into view. Oldham takes cover behind a tree as his sightline focuses in on Duey's 9mm.

"Sheriff's department, drop the gun!" Oldham shouts.

Duey squalls loud, incoherent words. He is edgy-eyed, trembling.

"Drop the gun!" Oldham commands again. "Drop it!"

Duey looks straight at him, his lungs bawling out a primitive yap.

A BLANCHED GREEN cabin leans left in a glen of naked oaks, fern-tipped hangnails and desiccated piles of straw-dark leaves. From forty feet away, Crabtree keeps his hands on his rifle as he studies the small structure, watching its slanted tin roof, two smudged windows and half-teetering screen door. His partner, Calaveras County Sheriff's Detective Chad Poortinga, carefully moves up to the wooden steps of the cabin's deck and past an old rusty barbecue embedded in the dirt.

They see their suspect move through a window before they

call him out with guns drawn. Thirty-year-old Kyle Hicks comes through the door without a struggle. The detectives handcuff him. Hicks is their suspect in stealing eight hundred feet of copper wire and a number of power tools, but as Crabtree and Poortinga move into the cabin they find his sawed-off shotgun, his box of ammunition, his illegal knives and his supply of methamphetamine.

Realizing Hicks has broken into the cabin, the detectives are getting ready to locate the owner when words come over their radio that no officer wants to hear.

"All units, be advised, officer-involved shooting at—"

Crabtree looks at Poortinga. They know the threat. They hear the coordinates. They may be the closest unit to Oldham, and they don't know what is happening to him. The investigators grab Hicks' gun, ammunition and meth, rushing over to the Ford. Crabtree quickly takes the handcuffs off the suspect. "This is your lucky day," he says. "But we'll be back for you later."

The Explorer's hidden lights flare on. Poortinga puts his foot on the gas as they race up Sheep Ranch Road. The SUV's frame rocks on chapped, discolored patterns of asphalt winding through mud-riven hills. Crabtree remembers the phone call that had come to dispatch in the night from a man who was seeing things: Driving out to find Hicks, Crabtree had listened on his radio to Oldham getting directed to the same neighborhood for a "shots fired" call. Crabtree had experienced a nagging feeling his fellow officer was going out to meet someone seeing the shadow people. Now the garbled intermittent radio waves solidify that premonition under his ribs. Like many veteran deputies, Crabtree has witnessed the fusion of methamphetamine and sleeplessness reduce people to near animals. Whatever is happening at this moment, he tells himself, it is just spiraling out of control. The SUV takes another sharp turn, passing the high, broken rises of spiny greasewood. Both deputies keep their eyes on the windshield as they get closer to Highway 4.

IT HAPPENS in a fractal second. "Drop the gun!" Oldham orders. Duey suddenly turns and tries to lunge up the side of an embankment of red clay. Wet from a passing rain, the sloppy soil plows down under him. Duey collapses. Oldham charges from the tree to a telephone pole in a rush for wider cover. Vaulting up from the ditch, Duey wrenches his upper body, craning his gun back in Oldham's direction. There is a single rifle flash.

CRABTREE AND POORTINGA brake to a stop at the rear bumper of an empty cruiser. They see Calaveras County Sheriff's Sergeant Rachelle Whiting standing next to Oldham. The two detectives get out, walking up the curved ascent. Kevin Duey lays in an earthen gutter clogged with random twigs and pinecones. The investigators stand over him. Their eyes hone in on the 9mm pistol resting on pebbles near a utility box. The crystal meth pipe is nestled in Duey's sweats. Spent 9mm shell casings are scattered across the driveway. A forty-eight-hour investigation lies ahead of the Sheriff's Department, but one question is already obvious: What would have happened if Duey had emerged from the woods minutes before while the children were at the bus stop? Or what if he had kept firing into the populated houses on the street? By virtue of pulling up, Oldham had apparently given him a new target, diverting the gunfire.

The detectives crouch down to identify the body. They are trying to find a wallet without moving its position, and that's when they see it—an electronic ankle bracelet monitor strapped to his leg.

TRUTHS OF AMERICAN justice are hard to see behind curtains of political posturing and financial gain; though sometimes a player on the stage breaks with the agreed upon script. Not long after this meth-fueled moment of violence under the trees in Arnold, California, United States Attorney General Eric Holder will give a speech acknowledging the nation's incarceration paradigm is "unsustainable." The words of the top law enforcement official in the U.S. speaking openly about prison overcrowding will go ringing through a crowded field of police, prosecutors, defense attorneys, victims, suspects, families and judges grappling with the question of how to protect communities without intentionally feeding humans into what Holder will describe as "a vicious cycle of poverty, criminality and incarceration." The United States currently has the highest incarceration rate, per capita, in the world, according to King's College in London. Between 1982 and 2011, the federal prison population quadrupled in size, while its percentage of violent offenders dropped from thirty-four percent to seven percent.

State prison populations mirror the federal trend. The number of inmates in California and Illinois tripled over the past sixteen years, while Alabama's prison population quadrupled between 1990 and 2000 alone. Many victims' rights organizations argue that the mandatory sentencing laws influencing this incarceration boom are essential to championing dignity and compassion for innocent victims whose lives have been shattered. At the same time, an abundance of law enforcement experts stress that continuing to choke off the influx of drugs—the arrests around which put a tremendous strain on prisons—remains the most direct way to combat property crime, gang violence and human exploitation. Polls suggest that a majority of Americans agreed with these sentiments in the past, supporting laws and policies that coincided with steadily dropping crime rates. However, California, Illinois and Alabama are among the states that now find themselves dangling on the edge of a moral and financial precipice. California has been found guilty by the U.S. Supreme Court of violating prisoners' constitutional rights. Illinois and Alabama are trying to avoid the same fate.

California lawmakers passed Realignment to change the equation, hoping local police officers, probation agents, addiction specialists, ministers and community leaders would be better equipped to rehabilitate criminals from their own neighborhoods than the failing state system, which currently has a seventy percent recidivism rate. California's Realignment was billed as being smarter, rather than weaker, on crime.

But just months into the Golden State's Realignment, opposition is rising. Numerous county jails across the state are receiving twice as many convicts to house than officials had estimated. Internal investigations and grand jury reports are finding that Realignment has caused some county jails to become unnecessarily dangerous facilities. Numerous jurisdictions are beginning to experience state prison convicts, now serving local terms, filing lawsuits over conditions in antiquated jails. It was such legal actions against the state's prisons that originally triggered Realignment's inmate-shift. More than a few county supervisors have declared California's new experiment a litigious and monetary shell game. In one county, sheriff's officials have openly expressed concerns that probation officials are re-writing policies in ways that impede other law enforcement agencies from searching Realignment offenders on the new supervision, creating unreliable data around the local successes and failures. And further complicating the picture is the scant mention of the word "victim" by California lawmakers. Leading victims' rights attorneys claim there is a legal paradox around Realignment: Under California's victims' rights initiative, Marcy's Law, all victims of crime have a state constitutional right to not see their perpetrator's prison sentence substantially reduced to alleviate prison overcrowding. A debate now continues over whether California's Realignment plan amounts to statutory law overriding the state constitutional rights of victims.

And the policy confusion in California is spreading through many parts of the nation. Illinois, Alabama and Louisiana are each windows into the paradoxes Americans face when trying to bolster public safety and support victims' rights only to run into a wall of reality—that being the question of what degree a society can pursue such goals without abandoning constitutional protections, moral principals and financial sustainability?

And so two rural county homicide detectives stand under the towering pine trees, peering down at a dead man, fixing their eyes on what is supposed to be a protective frontline in California's great new experiment with public safety. The nylon strap and plastic box. The electronic ankle bracelet. Technology's triumph in containing human fallibility. The investigators know the state's Realignment law has made cutting off ankle monitors a simple violation worth six months, at most, in a county jail; and at this moment correctional officials are tracking a one-hundred-eighteen percent jump in parolees cutting their bracelets off since Realignment passed. Kevin Duey did not even pry his bracelet off before his shooting episode. He simply brought it along for the ride. The detectives are staring at more than a device on a motionless leg, they are staring at an open question for everyone in California's landscape of crime, punishment and rehabilitation: Is prison overcrowding increasingly linked to more crime on the streets? And, if so, are any leaders looking past political talking points to bring the genuine failures and inequities paralyzing America's modern concept of justice to light?

CHAPTER 2

American Greybar

JOHN MAKI AND his staff were not in Dixon, Illinois during the moment of horror; but six years later, as their nonprofit fought to close what it deemed an inhumane super-maximum security prison on the other side of the state, what happened in Dixon was with them nearly every step of the way.

Dixon Correctional Center holds down a north border of the little Midwestern city that shares its name. The prison houses more than two thousand men. For years its cells have formed a concrete appendage of the quiet neighborhoods beyond: Prisoners walking its yards glimpse a smattering of farmhouses along the grassy lane of North Brinton Avenue. In the struggling "rust belt" of northern central Illinois—once the tool-manufacturing capital of the world—the jobs the prison provides keep Dixon from mirroring the window-snapped factory husks and half-desolated main streets that rot just miles down the river.

Spring mornings often flare bright over the city's welcome arch, an icon from World War I cresting below a Queen Anne church spire and the teal dome of an old justice hall. Early sunrays suffuse the National Bank's hundred-year-old bricks, its fifth story the highest rooftop in the valley, with the light glinning west down the red, white and fire-ant facades of First Street. Daybreak in Dixon is bygone stone seared in radiance, the nick of flatiron shadows from overhangs. A river splits the city— low, wide and moving with a cerulean slowness bluer than the cascading light above the maple trees along its banks.

But Dixon was not sunny on the unforgettable day. On that morning there were rain clouds. On that day, everything was different. Around noon, a 29-year-old female psychologist for the prison was at work inside X-House, the four-winged, maximum-security unit holding Illinois' most mentally deteriorated inmates. X-House is the newest building on the grounds: Its bare oblate brickwork is a design of crimson brutalism, starkly opposed to the Georgian architecture of the housing units, or the steeple-rise of the hall's colonial cupola lifting against the fields. According to legal records, the psychologist was in X-House when she was called to a prisoner's cell to "discuss an issue he was having." Watching her within the painted cavern of gray blocks and rust-red steel was John Spires. Despite being a serial rapist serving a two hundred and forty year sentence, Spires moved freely through the X-House hallways as he carried out his janitorial duties. His eyes were stalking the psychologist. Without any warning, Spires rushed over, grabbed her by the hair, held a makeshift knife to her throat and dragged her into a nearby closet.

A leaden shield rolled across the sky, raw over the choppy slate of the river and dark soil of the south-facing fields. Trucks coasted down Galena Avenue. They went bumping past a turn for the childhood home of Ronald Reagan and then the frontier opera house converted for silent pictures in the 1920s. Locals chatted over coffee at Books on First, a cozy den of tomes with a busy espresso bar. No one dreamed that, at that moment, Spires was barricading the door of the storage room inside X-House. When the inmate had firmly trapped his victim inside with him, he bound her with tape at the hands, ankles and mouth.

A twenty-five hour hostage crisis ensued while Spires promised correctional officers he would kill the psychologist if they came through the door. During the chaos, Spires brutally raped his victim.

At 1:30 p.m. on May 12, Spires finally grew hungry enough to allow officers to pass a tray of food to him, the contents of which were drugged. The woman he'd been torturing was rushed to a nearby hospital.

In the following weeks, journalist Jim Butts of *The Dixon Telegraph* attempted to get answers about how Spires so easily captured his victim. Butts also broke the story that, on the same day Spires attacked the psychologist, three files had been delivered to Dixon-area prosecutors involving assaults on correctional officers. Butts also knew that just weeks before the hostage situation was triggered, guards at Dixon had publicly warned that an escape, or the murder of an employee, was inevitable due to low officer staffing. Now the newshound pushed for more answers. While management at Dixon's prison was cooperative, Butts and his colleagues were rebuffed by their superiors at the Illinois Department of Corrections.

"Dixon Correctional Center employees complained publicly in April about understaffing at the prison, faulty equipment and blind spots in hallways," *The Dixon Telegraph* reported in December of that year. "Sauk Valley Newspapers have been trying to determine...why the warnings of prison guards a month earlier were not heeded. Working through the process outlined by the Illinois Freedom of Information Act, this newspaper has repeatedly requested information from the Illinois Department of Corrections about the incident...In response, the IDOC has either denied the requests or given out as little information as possible."

Prosecutors eventually told a Lee County jury that Spires premeditated every detail of the kidnap and rape from considering what objects could barricade the closet door to planning where he could hide his knife while on janitor duty.

The jury sentenced Spires to life without the possibility of parole.

Spires, then forty-nine, was sent to Tamms Correctional Center, a super-maximum security prison in southern Illinois. Clad in an escapee's green and yellow jumpsuit, he spent all but one hour a day in a seven by twelve-foot cinder-block cell. His single break between sunrise and sundown was wandering a twelve by thirty-foot concrete vault, slightly lit by an open section of sky. He was not allowed phone calls or conversations with other inmates. Occasionally Spires was escorted into a locked pod the size of a phone booth to watch television through re-enforced glass. Such moments were a reward for good behavior.

It was such conditions—for all inmates at Tamms—that led John Maki and his staff at the John Howard Association to publicly challenge the facility. Founded in 1901, the Illinois-based JHA is one of the only independent groups that monitors prison conditions. In 2010, a year after John Spires arrived at Tamms, a delegation from the JHA made an inspection of the prison. The nonprofit's ensuing report blasted Tamms for what it characterized as a "regime of sensory deprivation and social isolation." JHA monitors took particular aim at a discipline measure known as extended property reduction, which involved leaving inmates in entirely empty cells for days at a time "wearing nothing but a paper napkin." The report concluded that a widespread phenomena of inmates engaging in self-mutilation at Tamms was a direct result of psychological injury from harsh conditions.

In July of 2010, U.S. District Court Judge G. Patrick Murphy came to a similar conclusion, ordering that inmates at Tamms be given the formal right to contest any transfer to the prison.

By April of 2012, Illinois Governor Pat Quinn announced it was time the public had "a rendezvous with reality" regarding the state's prison overcrowding, as well as the $1.3 billion its penitentiaries were draining annually from the state's hemorrhaging general fund. One of Quinn's immediate plans was to close eight prisons in Illinois, which was forecasted to save the state $60 million the following year. Tamms became a primary target. The John Howard Association loudly advocated closing Tamms, pointing out taxpayers were spending $64,000 a year on each inmate held at Tamms—the most expensive incarceration rate in Illinois.

"Tamms was specially designed to hold people without human contact," Maki says. "That kind of practice destroys a human's mind. I have a lot of respect for correctional officers. They're the ones who are in there; but there was this idea with some of the officers that—whether it was reality or not—Tamms was a good threat to keep the peace in the overall correctional system. Absolutely no inmate wanted to go to Tamms. But I think the practices they used go too far, even if they were useful. On a profound level, what was wrong about Tamms is not about the institution itself but about the kind of society we are: Destroying a person's mind is not a valid form of punishment. Everyone needs a safeguard against highly dangerous inmates, but this was not the answer…Now we have to come up with an alternative that respects human life but also protects the officers, staff and inmates."

In July of 2012, Illinois chapters of the American Federation of State, County and Municipal Employees pushed back against Governor Quinn's move to close the prisons. The union held a meeting in Chicago, later posted on YouTube, in which they predicted violence would escalate in prisons after facilities such as Tamms were shuttered. Support for the union's warnings came from an unlikely voice: The knife-wielding sexual terrorist John Spires. With a camera rolling, Lori Laidlaw, a supervisor at Dixon Correctional Center, read a letter Spires had penned from the walls of Tamms.

"To put me back into a regular prison setting, the safety of others and myself will be in danger," Spires reflected. "I don't trust myself. A place like Tamms is needed. Just look at all of the other max joints…they are all in an uproar because they know—they meaning the inmates—that there's nothing that can be done to them if Tamms closes. So what do they have to fear or lose if an officer or inmate is killed? There have been no officer deaths since Tamms opened. And now you want to put all of us murderers and assaulters back into regular population? Don't you remember why you opened Tamms to begin with?"

Many of Spires' points were soon channeled into a lawsuit the union filed to halt the closure of Tamms on the grounds it would put the lives of correctional officers and prison employees at risk. The Illinois Supreme Court ultimately ruled Governor Quinn had the authority to close eight prisons, including Tamms.

In August 2012, John Spires was transferred out of Tamms. Months later the prison went out of operation.

The closure of a handful of prisons did little to solve Illinois' challenges with prison overcrowding. The state's facilities were designed to house thirty-four thousand inmates. By the start of 2012, they were holding roughly forty-eight thousand. The John Howard Association continued inspections of various prisons and reported finding some with broken windows and birds flying over floors laden with mice and cockroach infestations. The one hundred-year-old buildings were cold in the winter and stifling in the summer. More striking to Maki, a number of the prisons were engaging in "California-style" double-bunking in dorms—in a few cases triple-bunking—which created emotional boilerplates for fights and riots. Educational and rehabilitative efforts were few and operating on skeleton crews: Inmates with more than twenty years on their sentence could not access the programs, so they spent most of their time in cells. The JHA issued a number of reports, asserting these conditions made inmates more likely to commit new crimes once released. According to Maki, the investigations prompted "a few cosmetic changes" though the main problems with crowding and high recidivism remained daunting.

A civil action was filed in June of 2012 by the Uptown People's Law Center, charging that two Illinois prisons had interiors covered in mold, rust-colored water in their drinking fountains and clogged pipes leading to unflushed toilets for weeks at a time. Attorney Alan Mills told *The Illinois Times* that conditions were worse in these facilities than anything he'd read about in California. Much like John Maki and Governor Quinn, Mills became convinced Illinois was on the same collision course with the United States Supreme Court that California had just been on.

The path to California's great experiment in criminal justice began in 2001 when prisoners filed the class action lawsuit Plata vs. Schwarzenegger. After listening to six days of testimony in 2005, U.S. District Court Judge Thelton Henderson issued a series of factual findings in which he called the California prison medical care system "awful," "broken beyond repair" and directly responsible for an inmate dying "every six to seven days." Henderson also made it clear that the lawsuit had drawn his attention to the fact that California's prison population had grown by five hundred percent since 1980. In 2009, a panel of federal judges ruled the only way for California to achieve constitutional treatment of its convicts was by reducing its prison population by more than one hundred and thirty percent. In January of 2011, California's Attorney General, Jerry Brown, was elected for the second time in his life to the governorship. The lawsuit against the state's department of corrections was renamed Plata vs. Brown. Hesitant to open a floodgate for thirty thousand convicts pouring onto the streets, Brown's administration fought the ruling all the way to the U.S. Supreme Court. In May of that year, the high court ruled California's treatment of prisoners was equal to cruel and unusual punishment and thus violated the Eighth Amendment of the Constitution.

Brown responded to the prisoners' victory by championing

California Assembly Bill 109, soon to be known more famously as Realignment. The law funnels thousands of newly convicted criminals to county jails and probation departments rather than state prison.

The legal drama in California did not go unnoticed in Illinois.

"We use California as a kind of boogie man," Maki acknowledges. "We don't want to get where California is; but I'm concerned we're heading that direction…The Illinois Department of Corrections currently has a budget of $1.3 billion a year. It spends two percent of that on criminal rehabilitation programs. That tells you mathematically we're not doing what we need to make the inmates better here. I think that number tells you everything you need to know."

From Maki's perspective, the reasons for Illinois' packed penitentiaries are legion and include a flourishing prison industry and politically popular "tough on crime" sentencing laws. Governor Pat Quinn's 2010 decision to eliminate an early release program for inmates demonstrating good conduct is also a move the JHA questions: The program was axed after hard-hitting newspaper investigations proved a number of prisoners released under it were back in custody in a matter of days or weeks for new crimes.

Now, as news-watchers in Illinois observe California grind through a legally brutal year, Quinn and his state's general assembly have passed a law reinstating a new version of early release program; though this one mandates inmates serve at least sixty days of their sentence. The John Howard Association is pushing lawmakers to go further, urging them to use new inmate threat matrixes to determine which men and women need to be in cells and which are appropriate for community-based forms of corrections.

"For the last thirty years we've seen the concepts of prison and punishment as synonymous," Maki observes. "And that's what's happened across the country. Prison is one form of punishment but it's not the only form. We need to de-couple those ideas. There are other forms of punishment."

But for victims advocates in Illinois, the John Howard Association's push for more diversionary programs and alternative sentencing sounds a lot like California's Realignment law. Throughout 2012, any journalism connoisseur could go online and find ample disturbing news stories out of California, especially around convicts being monitored—or not monitored— under the counties' new Post Release Community Supervision program, or PRCS. The development of the PRCS option puts thousands of convicts coming out of state prison under the supervision of county probation agents and programs rather than experienced parole officers. The program is a lynchpin in making the state prison populations work under Realignment.

Within months of Realignment passing, a click of the mouse brought the headlines up: An armed carjacking in Hemet by a 27-year-old reportedly on PRCS; a girl in Stockton bludgeoned to the point of being wheelchair-bound and mentally disabled for life by a boyfriend on PRCS. A murder in Richmond by a young man who law enforcement claims was on PRCS. Before California's Realignment, all of these suspects would have been monitored by highly experienced parole agents capable of sending them back to prison.

Maki knows that pushing Illinois policy makers toward

the community correction model means combating anecdotal reports coming out of California. But Maki's been here before. The John Howard Association's drive to close Tamms prison was haunted by the deeds—and later the direct warnings—of the brutal serial rapist John Spires. Though one inmate in a landscape of institutions, Spires had caused untold pain, trauma and horror. In the face of a prison-overcrowding crisis forty years in the making, Maki urges people to use logic to fight against anxiety.

"When someone on parole commits a heinous crime, it's jarring," he admits. "That's a common response. I feel it too. But that's also the nature of criminal justice. You'll never have a perfect system. You're still dealing with human beings who will sometimes make awful decisions. But when these things happen, attention focuses on that one case, and breathes the whole system through that one case, and that's a mistake. It's very understandable, but it's bad policy."

KATIE TEMPESTA LOOKS at the video lenses tracking her. She listens to the rapid shutter-snaps of cameras at her side. With the dome of California's Capitol building looming above, Katie's fingers tighten on her mother's portrait, which is pressed near her heart. A cool October breeze is everywhere, and Katie has no way to know that in a matter of months her mother's killer will look across an anonymous Fresno courtroom and lock eyes with her—and then he'll smile.

On this afternoon, Katie has yet to face those deranged eyes. She stands before the media as a 21-year-old mother and fulltime college student. Her own mom, Lisa, was also a college student, taking courses in Fresno alongside Katie for the last three years. Lisa was just a few credits shy of earning her paralegal certificate. Watching her mother inch closer to a new profession in those days, Katie could already see an alternate but familiar future: Lisa had a passion for helping the downtrodden in her central city neighborhood. Though short on cash, she often fed the homeless and constantly offered favors to struggling friends. The paralegal degree would come, but Katie understood her mother would still be living in the tiny studio apartment on Van Ness Avenue, her kitchen tabletop piled with stacks of legal filings, work she'd then be doing for free on behalf of locals living in poverty or trapped in desperate situations. Katie knew that—unlike many women who achieve a major career change through hard work—it simply wasn't in Lisa's nature to make money at it. The image still makes Katie smile: After all the classes and sacrifice, her mother would still be struggling; but she would finally be happy.

Lisa's generosity would soon bring a one-man train of meth-fueled aggression to her doorstep in the form of Michael Cockrell. The path to their meeting started when Lisa befriended a young woman named Jennifer Gonzales. Roughly the same age as Katie, Gonzales was having difficulties and needed a place to stay. Lisa offered the girl a sleeping bag and air mattress on her studio floor. It was one of Lisa's vintage gestures of compassion. And it would be her last.

Gonzales was friends with Cockrell, who lived in an apartment complex across the back alley from Lisa's patio. Cockrell had recently been sent to prison on charges of domestic battery. Given a three-year prison term, he walked out of custody after serving only six months, transferred to PRCS. While beating a pregnant woman would seem on its face to be a violent offense, the mechanics of PRCS allowed Cockrell to be running the streets with little to no supervision.

It is unknown why Cockrell came to Lisa's apartment in the dark morning hours looking for Gonzales. What Katie can envision are the quiet motions her mother was going through when the killer arrived. Lisa would have woken up. She would have walked her dog as she started to cook breakfast. She would then have hunkered down over her mounds of legal homework. Katie will never know which step of the ritual Lisa was in when neighbors suddenly heard her screaming, "You need to stop!"

Responding to a 911 call, Fresno police officer Jonathan Linzey pulled up to the alley behind Lisa's studio. He had just gotten out of his patrol car when he saw Jennifer Gonzales in a narrow walkway between a retaining wall and the whitewashed side of the complex. She was bleeding from an array of knife wounds. Linzey moved through the tunnel-like path toward Lisa's back door. He didn't make it. The Fresno police would later tell Katie the story blow by blow: Cockrell hurled out of a blind spot to stab Officer Linzey in the head. Blood streaming down, Linzey fought with Cockrell as two more Fresno police officers ran out of their braking patrol cars. They struggled to cuff the crazed, screaming assailant. One fired his Taser. The scene became shouts and plasma—a fight erupting on the periphery of crimson spatters that led into the apartment where Lisa laid sprawled between the kitchen and living room with more than fifteen stab wounds to her neck and face.

Katie is still months away from sitting down at Cockrell's pretrial hearing where she will see his shaven head has sprouted into a thick bush his eyes tilt under—mousey and deep-set into the bone-diamond brow constantly bearing down on Katie. Cockrell will look at her before flashing a clear, unmistakable grin.

But at this moment, now, there are only the news cameras training in, their lenses framing Katie next to Lynne Brown, a new woman she is drawing strength from.

Lynne Brown does not fit the image most California politicians would have envisioned as the person leading the charge against Realignment. A blue collar mother of two, Lynne's knowledge of crime comes from working in the security industry and being married to Dwight Brown, a Sacramento sheriff's sergeant who's worked the most violent beats in the region. A marriage to "D" Brown and friendships with his fellow deputies has left Lynne with one undying motto: "The truth is in the streets." She was mortified when she started learning the mechanics of Assembly Bill 109. For Lynne, the idea of putting thousands of convicted burglars, drug dealers, stalkers and identity thieves onto the streets rather than state prison could only have one outcome. She formed Advocates for Public Safety as a watchdog group for the Realignment plan.

Lynne knows the meaning of anecdotal evidence. She understands why Americans see it as a qualifier. She accepts that the public has its doubts about any warning labeled a random, worst-case scenario. But, staring at Katie holding her dead mother's picture against the wind, Lynne wonders exactly how many victims it takes before something officially transitions from "anecdotal" to a pattern of impact.

This afternoon marks Katie's debut as a human face for Advocates for Public Safety; but it is also the genesis of a growing bond between the college student and Lynne Brown, a mentor who will encourage her argument papers and into entering student speech competitions. As the connection between the women grows, Lynne, whose own children are only slightly younger than Katie, will recognize through maternal instincts that Katie is being affected by Cockrell's court dates. With the numbing shock of Lisa's murder wearing away, Katie comes closer to the details of each knife stroke. Her tough exterior will show signs of cracking. And Lynne will understand that the journey for Katie is just beginning, with a shadow of visceral blood and violence waiting at the end of the line.

Standing at the state Capitol, Katie plans to be strong; or at least strong enough to use the details of her mother's death to expose what she and Lynne see as the most emphatic lie about California's Post Release Community Supervision program—the claim that criminals managed under it are all "nonviolent, nonsexual and non-serious" offenders. While this assertion has been a key talking point for champions of the law it ignores the fact Realignment created an "exclusion list" of crimes that allows convicts coming out of state prison who committed offenses on the index to be eligible for PRCS rather than strict parole. Inmates walking out of the gates convicted of felony stalking, brandishing a firearm at a police officer, solicitation of murder and felony child abuse are all now under the charge of county probation offices used to dealing with much lower-level offenders. The charge that originally put Michael Cockrell behind bars, and eventually landed him on the "exclusion list," was felony domestic violence. Fresno County probation officers apparently did not detect the meth-induced hysteria he was falling into during the weeks leading up to Lisa's murder. The list deemed Cockrell nonviolent. Lynne has focused on this subterfuge in the law during recent speaking engagements.

"People are being misled about who's in their community,"

she says. "People in positions of authority are deceiving the public about who these 'non, non, nons' really are. Realignment is intentionally confusing. It seems like its authors count on people not having time to invest in their busy lives when it comes to learning about what it actually does…Telling the truth is a transparency issue and it's an ethics issue."

Despite the fact that Lynne Brown does support criminal rehabilitation, many Realignment supporters are attacking Advocates for Public Safety with the charge of "fear-mongering" through selected, anecdotal stories. Realignment defenders are quick to make the same claim about journalists, sending scathing opinion pieces to the editorial sections of those reporters' newspapers. When the *Los Angeles Times* ran a story about the alleged crimes of Ka Pasasouk, the California Department of Corrections and Rehabilitation resorted to a similar tactic. Pasasouk was arrested for possession of methamphetamine in 2012. Despite having a violent criminal history, he was sent to Los Angeles County custody and supervision. Three months later, Pasasouk allegedly murdered four people in a Northridge Boarding House. When the *Times* questioned whether the slayings might have been avoided if Pasasouk had been supervised by experienced state parole agents rather than county probation officers, the department of corrections' spokesman Luis Patino issued a statement accusing the *Times* of using the Northridge killings to "perpetuate myths about Realignment."

As the first full year of California's Realignment wrenches on, newspaper readers continue to see a cycle of beat coverage and critic response: A journalist writes a story about someone who would have otherwise been under state custody or supervision committing new crimes, and then Realignment supporters fire off opinion pieces accusing the reporter of sensationalism and reckless coverage. Lynne Brown faces many of the same criticisms. And it is true that random evidence can't illuminate phenomenon unless bolstered by statistical support. But in the world of flesh, blood and crime tape, Lynne wonders exactly how many confirmed tragedies have to be documented before the cases shift from being considered "anecdotal evidence" to California's new reality. It's a question that haunts her maternal core whenever she glances at Katie during Cockrell's murder proceedings, seeing the girl's energetic beauty blunted, her doe eyes dazed with tears, all from getting closer and closer to the unrelenting gore of those photographs of her mother on the apartment floor.

For Lynne Brown it all comes back to one fundamental: "The truth is in the streets."

CHAPTER 3

February, San Andreas, California: Testify

THE MEPHITIC TANG of a courthouse from the 1960s burns in his senses.

Calaveras County Sheriff's Detective Josh Crabtree sits in a hallway as the murder trial he's spent eight months preparing for finally begins. The investigator is barred from hearing testimony before he's called to give his own account; and as the morning commences he can only speculate how his star witness—Kevin Patton—will perform in front of the jury.

It started with screams.

Patton was lying on the couch in his singlewide trailer as a late June heat baked the outskirts of Valley Springs. A van rolled by his window. In its passenger seat was James Livezey, a 6-foot mountain who had been buying and using methamphetamine around the county for decades. Livezey was clear-headed on this night, having recently quit his addiction under the weight of terminal brain cancer. His girlfriend Angela Sullivan wasn't as eager to give up the head dust. Sullivan was the mother of Livezey's baby, though she reportedly did little to watch their child during her spouse's barrage of cancer treatments, often disappearing for long periods of time to meet with her drug connections. Livezey would later sum it up to detectives with the blunt admission, "I've got an old lady who wants to do crank all the time."

The sun's wheel was buried on a summit behind the churches, pulling a shadow line down the eastern hills, washing dim pitches of yolk-yellow grass and scattered warts of granite. The town's lamps were blinking on. Late-hour light moved over shingled rooftops, Castle Rock trailers and tall, flaring oleanders that billowed against fences. The ridge tops beyond Highway 26 were stroked in the falling sun, their scrub brush and oaks glowing in the same aerial shimmer that opened a passing blush on the clouds. Livezey was walking down a street when someone told him Angela Sullivan was inside Marvin Brown's trailer at the Sequoia Rose Mobile Home Park. Brown was a thin, 52-year-old meth addict covered in burn scars.

The moments ticked away.

Kevin Patton heard a woman screaming. He rushed outside, ambling along a sluice of dead bushes that jutted under his front window. His friend Reanna Silveira was in the road crying out, "He's hitting him! He's hitting him!"

Patton started jogging. He crossed the dry tresses of a hanging willow tree and the webbed panels of a singlewide with boarded windows silvered strangely under the streetlamp. The sky was nearly black. A kindling blue dusk still traced over the western hills. Patton went by Silveira, marching onto the track of gravel that curved for Marvin Brown's unit. The entrance came into view, and on approach Patton saw two figures in the open doorway: Brown lay on his back, as if his spine was nailed to the floor, his feet pointed out toward the warm night air. A large man hovered above Brown with his shoulders turned. The man was bent down with his arms rocking a maddened cadence, either strangling Brown's sinewy neck or pummeling his fragile face.

"Hey stop!" Patton shouted. "Stop!"

IT WAS THAT forceful utterance that has now, in this moment, this morning, brought Kevin Patton to Calaveras County's courthouse.

"And what happened then?" Deputy District Attorney Seth Matthews asks from behind the prosecutor's table.

Patton settles into the witness stand. A creased, collared shirt holds loose to his narrow frame. His short hair is combed back, its dark shine matching a pencil-thin goatee below sparse, slightly tanned cheekbones. There's a hardened leanness in his face as he replies, "Guy turned around, and then he started coming at me." The words are direct, summoned from Patton's strained, airy drawl. The witness adds, "And then, he just said to me, 'the bitch should have stayed home.'"

Matthews nods. "So you were walking up," the prosecutor observes, "and you yell at the man, and he turns around and walks out, is that right?"

"Yeah."

"Where did he go next?"

"He started walking down the stairs, coming at me."

"How close?"

"Probably within three feet."

"And what was he doing at that point?"

"At the time he was real angry, you know what I mean?" Patton recalls. "We kind of squared-up." He hesitates and then brings the scene back with the slow western rhythm in his throat: "We were facing each other. And then he just said it again, 'Bitch should have stayed home.'…Reanna jumped in between us. She said to the defendant, 'this is my friend, leave him alone, leave him alone.' It all happened in a few seconds."

"Did you ask him any questions?"

"Yeah," Patton says flatly. "I asked him, "What the hell are you doing, man? What did you do?'… He just started walking away. I seen him head toward the van that was parked outside."

Matthews has Patton walk the jury step-by-step through what happened next. The witness talks about grabbing Marvin Brown's wrist and searching for a pulse. He remembers dropping his face to Brown's mouth without feeling a trace of breath blowing back. He recounts lifting Brown's scarred, flaccid body, carrying it to the edge of the road. He tells Matthews about how he had started blowing oxygen into Brown's mouth while pumping on his heart. He describes Reanna Silveira running back to his own trailer, trying in vain to find a cell phone. He remembers throwing the keys for his roommate's Toyota to Silveira and demanding she bring the car around. Patton keeps talking. He's running through all of it again: Seeing Silveira pull the vehicle up to the side of Brown's lifeless form just before she was overtaken by a spun onslaught of anxiety. Silveira was panicking. She was frantic. Patton was forced to load Marvin Brown into the back of the Toyota by himself. Patton says aloud that Silveira was so paralyzed with shock that he turned to Angela Sullivan—the girl for whom Brown had been laid low—and ordered her into the car's back seat to watch the victim. Patton takes the courtroom through his desperate drive from the Sequoia Rose Mobile Home Park to the nearby Valley Springs fire station. He remembers rushing to the building of grey cinder block and midnight blue windows, pounding over and over on its front door. Patton tells the judge that when he realized no one was coming to help, he jumped back into the Toyota and sped down Highway 26 for Mark Twain Medical Center.

"And, as you were driving, is it fair to say you were yelling at the defendant's girlfriend, Miss Sullivan?" the prosecutor inquires.

A sharpness tightens in on Patton's eyes. "Yeah."

"Were you rude with her at all?"

"Yes."

"And is that because, as you were driving, you asked Miss Sullivan to do mouth-to-mouth resuscitation on Mr. Brown?"

"I asked her to breathe on his mouth," Patton responds. "I kept telling her to try to save his life; but she made it clear she wasn't into it. I mean, she wasn't going to do it."

"And, at some point on the way to the hospital, did you notice what Angela Sullivan was doing in the back seat with Mr. Brown?"

Patton's featherweight frame grows visibly tense: "Yeah. She was digging through his pockets...I was kind of paying attention to the road, but looking in my rearview mirror at the same time—she was getting into his pockets."

Matthews lets the image hang over the courtroom; and it does linger, alive in a span of silence under the echoes of disgust in Patton's tone, leaving the jurors to ponder if within those chaotic moments Angela Sullivan's main concern was getting her hands on any methamphetamine that might still be in her dying friend's pants.

The prosecutor returns to the other woman who was at the

killing scene. "Did you later ask Miss Silveira what happened that night?" he puts to the witness.

"She was crying on my chest about what had happened," Patton replies with even measure. "She said Marvin was struck from behind, that James grabbed him as his knees buckled and threw him to the floor."

Matthews concludes his examination, leaving the floor open to Ken Foley, one of Calaveras County's best-known criminal defense attorneys. Foley's voice launches on a calm sail at first. "Mr. Patton, how much did you have to drink that night?"

The witness ticks his head back. "Not much," he replies. "I was at work until 4:30 p.m. I got home at 5 p.m. Ms. Silveira was there with my roommate. They had been drinking all day together. I had a couple of beers and a glass of wine."

"And so it's your recollection," Foley says, rising from the defense table, bracing hard against his chronic back pain, "that you didn't spend three hours in the middle of the day with Ms. Silveira?"

"No, I was at work."

"Okay, let me ask you this question," the attorney goes on, his volume elevating. "If Ms. Silveira swore under oath that she was with you that day, drinking wine and beer for three hours during the afternoon, would she be a liar?"

"Yep."

"Is she a liar?"

Patton leans far forward. "If she says that I didn't work from 7:30 a.m. to 4:30 p.m., like I do every single day, five days a week,"—the jurors can hear a faint slap simmering in his pitch—"then she would be."

"Okay, so you were not drinking with her during the day?"

"No."

"And then in the evening you were drinking with her?"

"After work."

"And you were drinking wine?"

"I was drinking beer," Patton corrects him. "They were drinking wine. I had aaaiiieee glass of wine." He stares at Foley. With his drawl cracking strong, he adds, "It was shitty wine."

"Do you know of any reason why she would say she was with you that day?"

"She was with me that day. Just after 5 o'clock."

"Yeah, but why would she say she was with you during the early afternoon hours?"

"I have no idea why she would say that. I was at work."

"It's not true?"

"Not true."

"Okay," Foley reasons aloud, "So, if she says Livezey pushed Brown from behind?"

"But that's not what she told me."

Foley continues his thought: "So, if she says Livezey pushed Brown from behind, do you think that's true?"

"She didn't tell me he was pushed from behind," Patton fumes with his chin dipping and his eyes drilling into the attorney. "She said he was struck from behind."

"Alright, alright," Foley says. He begins thumbing through his notes. "On that evening of June 29, do you know how much Ms. Silveira had to drink and how much methamphetamine she had consumed before she came to get you at the trailer?"

"No, she didn't tell me about her using methamphetamine until afterwards because, at the time, I wasn't messing with no amphetamines. She knew I didn't like it around me."

"Did you have any idea what had been going on in the trailer?"

"About the fight that happened?" Patton asks, "Or about what her, Marvin and Angela were doing?"

"How about Angela Sullivan? Did you know what she was doing?"

"Yeah."

Foley's eyebrows make a grand lift along with his tenor. "What was she doing?"

"She was over there with Marvin Brown, smoking dope and doing his laundry," Patton answers with a quick, emphatic coldness.

"You knew that?"

"Not for sure. I never seen it with my own eyes."

"But you thought that?"

"Yep."

"Did you speak to Angela Sullivan that night?"

"I yelled at her."

"And what condition did she appear to be in?"

Patton takes a breath. "She didn't know what to do," he remembers. "She was just kind of lost."

"Did she appear out of it?"

"No, not 'out of it.' She just had no feelings."

"Is that because she was stoned from crank?"

"I don't know."

"Could be?" Foley fires at him.

"Could be," the witness parrots loudly.

"So, when you went there that night, into that room, did you know that they had all been doing meth?"

"Did I know they had been doing meth when I walked

into the room?" Patton asks himself so the jurors can hear. He pauses. The fine, slim line of his shoulder blades elevates under the dress shirt, his forehead dropping, his dry, wan brow training on Foley: "Well," he says with lifeless pupils, "I had a pretty strong suspicion."

Foley returns to his notes as he launches into questions about the condition of Brown's body when Patton arrived, as well as the manner in which he had loaded the dying man into the Toyota.

"And why didn't Miss Silveira go with you?" Foley inquires about the hospital trip.

"Because Miss Silveira was running around like a chicken with her head cut off," Patton answers. "She was freaking out."

"Did Miss Silveira tell you, in her revelation, that she had a warrant out for her?"

"Yeah."

"So, is that why she didn't go with you?'

"No, she was flipping out: She was hysterical."

"And did you know at the time she had been doing the same drugs as the other people?"

Patton sits back, his voice sinking with him. "Not at the time."

"But you know it now, right?" Foley observes, glancing up and then waiting. The witness keeps a chilled stare for a second and then slowly nods. Before the court reporter can tell Patton to enunciate, Foley conjures a new, urgent power in his volume. "And out of the three people who were in that trailer that night, who you know were smoking methamphetamine, one's dead, one was in a stupor and the other was running around, acting crazy?"

"Objection," the prosecutor calls out. "Argumentative."

The witness doesn't wait for the next question. "She was distraught," he snaps. "She'd just seen a man blasted from behind, who was down and laying there without a pulse," the airy agitation in Patton's throat is roughening, each word a jab, "a man who, was, her, friend."

Foley measures Patton for only an instance before asking, "The first time you spoke to law enforcement that day, you didn't reveal most of this story you just shared with us, did you? Was that intentional?"

"Yeah it was— it was a conscious decision."

"Why?"

"I was nervous at the time," Patton returns, his dark eyebrows jacking up. "I was living in a shit-hole neighborhood with a bunch of convicts, and I didn't know what I was going to do. Snitching is not fun, you know what I mean?" The jurors stare at him. "You know?" Patton continues to reflect, "being labeled a snitch? I had to think about what I was going to do."

He lets a small breath out: "But, in the end, what's right is right."

A journalist heads out of the courtroom and the assailing timber of Foley's next question dissipates when the door closes. Crabtree and Deputy Allen Serpa sit at a yardsale-type folding table placed randomly in the dreary hallway.

"Patton's holding up pretty well in there," the reporter tells them. "He's not taking anything from Foley. He was even coming back at him a few times."

Crabtree pulls his flu-fired eyes off the courthouse window. "Really?" he asks, looking up.

"I believe it," Serpa says quietly. "What can Foley do to him? At this point, he's got nothing to lose."

A silence settles over the cheap table. The officers stare vacantly into different corners of the hallway. One is clamming up with a head cold; the other is exhausted; and each knows that while the testimony beyond the door involves a meth clan from Valley Springs it captures just one sliver of the hundreds of addicts fueling nearly all of the burglaries, batteries, assaults, identify thefts and child abuse cases occupying files at their office. With the exception of Kevin Patton, who has himself struggled with methamphetamine, every other witness in the Livezey murder investigation is arguably a study in criminal thinking. For Crabtree and Serpa, encountering "criminal thinking" is in the fabric of their daily experience; but the term itself is now circulating mightily through California since the passage of its new law, AB 109. The law and the bigger issue of handling criminal thinking have started to pit public agencies, especially in Calaveras County, against one another.

A few weeks ago the drama played out publicly in the *Calaveras Enterprise* newspaper through a series of letters penned by clashing agency leaders. With Realignment transferring an enormous amount of job duties from the state's parole authority to fifty-eight different county probation offices, Calaveras's chief of probation, Teri Hall, weighed in on what she felt AB 109 means for the impoverished ranching community. Hall's letter examined California's recidivism rate for the very offenders her office would be in charge of rather than state prisons or state parole agents. She argued a sizable portion of the money Calaveras would be granted to offset Realignment should be spent on a research-validated day reporting center where offenders on Post Release Community Supervision would get guidance, instruction and support to change their lives.

"Napa County has experienced a twenty-three percent re-offense rate among their day reporting center graduates," Hall wrote. "This is much less than the state average which is seventy percent, while the national average is forty percent… Probation staff monitors offenders closely with daily check-ins, ongoing drug and alcohol testing, intensive case management and cognitive behavioral classes that target the reasons for criminal behavior."

The probation chief added in a clear rebuttal to views within Calaveras's sheriff's office: "We know that California's lack of effective local community corrections has been a major contributor to a system that relies heavily on incarceration. What we don't need is more of the same."

But the tone of the next letters suggested Hall was on a proverbial island. One statement was from Todd Fordahl, chief of the Angels Camp Police Department. Fordahl questioned the notion that Hall's proposal was a new or novel approach to handling local criminals. "The majority, if not all, of the programming that is being proposed at the 'Day-Use Reporting Center' is currently offered by the county," Fordahl observed. The chief then scrutinized the details of what Hall envisioned at her new center. "The idea of using limited funds to provide gift cards for this population, for doing what is expected of them, is a complete waste of the taxpayer's money," Fordahl emphasized. "I agree there is at least one philosophical difference between Ms. Hall and I, related to the idea of arming the probation officers that will be charged with supervising this population. Ms. Hall has expressed that she feels it sends the wrong message to the AB 109 population to have armed probation officers interacting with them. I believe that it is a safety issue for the probation officers, and for the public and other peace officers working with them."

Public criticism also came from Crabtree and Serpa's commander at the sheriff's office, Captain Jim Macedo, whose open letter charged that Hall had tried to write a policy barring sheriff's deputies and police officers from arresting PRCS offenders in the commission of a new crime unless they had permission from her department. Macedo stressed that Hall wanted her own personnel contacted before arresting PRCS offenders "even when a violation of the terms of probation are committed in the presence of a deputy sheriff."

The captain added, "When asked why we should agree to seek permission from the probation officer prior to making an arrest, we received the response that the arrest might interfere with the offender's treatment and rehabilitation. It's the sheriff's office's duty to protect the public from becoming victims of crimes. We are not going to be apologetic to offenders who commit crimes or violate terms and conditions of their probation. However, we are apologetic to the victims residing in this county who become victimized due to the negligence of this plan."

Macedo's command staff will later acknowledge Hall also wanted to implement a policy requiring sheriff's deputies and police officers to make "appointments" with PRCS offenders for home searches days before the searches occurred, thus rendering the checks—in the opinion of many—virtually meaningless. In the new paradigm of Realignment, beat cops are hyper-aware that the success of probation departments is measured by recidivism data and statistics around how many

PRCS offenders are re-arrested on fresh crimes or violations of their court orders.

The letters taking aim at Hall's Realignment plan came from more than law enforcement agencies: Kelli Fraguero, who runs Calaveras's shelter for domestic violence victims, penned a criticism that explored the ramifications of classifying criminals as "non-violent" when they have documented histories of violence. "This population has had a negative impact on peoples' lives," Fraguero wrote to the *Enterprise*. "Many victims wonder if the label 'non, non, non' will mean that authorities will not take seriously the possible threat posed by their return. In many cases the DUI arrest that sent an individual to prison was also an answered prayer of a battered spouse who was too terrified to report."

Within two months, Josh Crabtree's wife, Tammie, will share similar concerns as the head of Amador County's shelter for threatened women, telling a reporter, "It's just going to make even less victims come forward— they'll think, 'now I know there's no way they can protect me.'"

In the flurry of public letters and statements, Hall's only support came from Rita Downs, director of Calaveras County Behavioral Health Services. In a brief statement, Downs noted models like Hall's day reporting program had been used "successfully in other states to reduce recidivism."

But if Hall appears lonely within her own rural county she has philosophical allies at the state capitol and a clear mandate from the governor's office. That much is clear.

CRABTREE AND SERPA testify and then go back to their assignments. A few days pass. Foley calls Kevin Patton back to the witness stand. He asks Patton if it is true that he's currently being charged with a property crime by the same district attorney's office that's deemed him the star witness of the Livezey trial.

"I caught a case," Patton says.

"In the course of being prosecuted in that case," Foley probes, "have you had any conversations with the district attorney's office?"

"For that case?"

"Yes."

"No, I've just talked to my public defender," Patton tells him. "It's totally separate, what's going on."

"And so did it ever dawn on you that if you do a good job in this case, you might…?" Foley lets the question linger.

"I don't work like that, Mr. Foley, man," Patton replies. "What's right is right. If I do something, I accept my consequences. I don't ask nobody for favors. I earn my own way."

"That never crossed your mind?"

Patton looks at him. "Not one time, bud."

The questions end. Kevin Patton, the one witness to ignore Valley Springs' code of silence, will stand on his own with the jury, one way or the other.

Over the course of two weeks, jurors watch James Livezey's tumor-torqued movements, the confused, ragged lurching that fumbles him when trying to get from the jail's corridor to the defendant's table; and the courtroom is also decorated with the sight of Katherine Livezey, the extremely ill and frail mother of the accused. Despite her own health failing, Katherine manages to come to court each day to keep her battered eyes on the witnesses parading on and off the stand.

The jury heads into deliberation on a Friday. They return with a verdict the following Monday: James Livezey is found guilty of involuntary manslaughter rather than second-degree murder. Citing medical testimony that the defendant is not expected to live, Judge Edward M. Lacy sentences Livezey to a three-year prison term. But the real shock for the Calaveras County Sheriff's Department is still on the way: According to California's Realignment, manslaughter is no longer a violent crime under the law. Livezey, convicted of beating another man to death or breaking his neck in a fit of rage, is now a terminally ill cancer patient who belongs in the custody and care of one of the most under-funded sheriff's offices in California. It is now the duty of the county's jail staff to fight Livezey's brain tumor, to repeatedly transport him to U.C. Davis Medical Center seventy-five miles away, to deal with his brain-impaired fits of rage in a manner that will protect the county from the types of condemnations a federal court has brought down on the state's prisons. How it can be afforded, how it can be done, is unknown.

Five months go by. A heat wave grips the seared, browned hills of the county, carrying with it a new crime spree sheriff's deputies are thrust against; and Katherine Livezey, with her son still breathing under the weight of his tumor in a cell, passes away. Her funeral is held on a summer evening at Good Samaritan Church in Valley Springs. In time, the church's yard will be combed during an immense manhunt in the wake of 8-year-old Leila Fowler being stabbed to death inside her home, just up the road. The little girl's slaying will leave the entire

Valley Springs community chilled to the bone. But Katherine Livezey had just lived long enough to see the most brutal expression of death come into her family's sphere, this time branding one of their own. Katherine's funeral commences. The sun is still blinding on the church's plain, lifted crucifix, still throwing a sky-fired flaxen glow on the foxtails sweeping up in the oak bowers, until the lightsome heat glares on a harsh patchwork of growth and greasewood rolling back to the rooftops of town—back to the bowing wood fences, the primer car hoods and the rusted-out shed tops of the Sequoia Rose Mobile Home Park.

James Livezey is dying. At 42-years-old, his own world choked his brain to death.

CHAPTER 4

Legacies rising

IT'S A COLD Chicago afternoon as attorney Bryan Stevenson makes his way into the ballroom of the Sheraton Hotel and Towers, the tan, prosaic dimensions split by a bevy of men and women in suits. Stevenson is looking out at faces of the Illinois Judges Association: A member rises to the podium introducing him as the keynote speaker. There is a brief flight through Stevenson's accomplishments in thirty years of being a civil rights attorney, including winning the MacArthur Genius Fellowship, the Ford Foundation Visionary Award and The Roosevelt Freedom from Fear Award. The reformer slips past two long tables on the stage, each draped in cream-colored linen, each lined with judges looking down at their lunch plates.

Stevenson knows he is standing before vital players in the Illinois justice system, a landscape so burdened with mass incarceration many believe a reckoning between the state and the U.S. Supreme Court is inevitable. Stevenson is an expert on the problems that come with prison overcrowding. For most of his career he has worked in Alabama, a state with the third highest incarceration rate in the nation. Growing up in shadowed memories of lynchings and the residual terrorism of Jim Crow laws, Stevenson is not a man who believes crimes against communities should be ignored. Yet the civil rights litigator has also experienced three decades of one perpetual complication: The reality that weaving crime into the deepest fibers of American politics has, in his view, created an erratic tendency for blind reaction. Stevenson has seen its consequences, to the point where collective logic gives way to labeling 13-year-old boys from poor neighborhoods "super predators." He has also witnessed men and women sentenced to life without parole for three non-violent offenses. Worst yet, he watches daily as more and more prisons in the nation reach a breaking point, all while private corporate boards work to bring profits from the crisis directly to Wall Street.

Stevenson begins to speak to the judges, explaining that his entire career in the courts has been one prolonged battle with an invisible force—an American culture of hysteria.

He starts with the story he knows best, his own.

Stevenson became the man he is today on death row. In 1985, the fresh-faced attorney graduated Harvard University and began working for the Southern Center for Human Rights in Atlanta, Georgia. One of Stevenson's main assignments was reviewing cases of inmates sentenced to death, mainly by lethal injection. It only took a dozen face-to-face conversations with these men to open Stevenson's eyes to a realization that startled him: Despite the U.S. Supreme Court issuing a ruling in 1963 that guaranteed every American accused of a crime adequate defense, many counties across the Deep South were doing little or nothing to provide that safeguard. Georgia had no statewide public defender system. During Stevenson's first year in Atlanta, his fellow attorneys at SCHR listened to the vice president of the Georgia Trial Lawyers Association describe the condition of public defense with an observation called the mirror test—"you put a mirror under the court-appointed lawyer's nose, and if the mirror clouds up, that's adequate defense."

In a nation that would quickly see three hundred and twelve inmates sentenced to death suddenly exonerated by new DNA techniques, Stevenson was meeting countless death-row prisoners who had lacked any real public defense. For the young attorney, the revelation of how indifferent the American justice system can be to its own purported laws and values was deeply transformative.

In 1989, Stevenson took the helm of a new non-profit group, the Equal Justice Initiative. Based in Montgomery, Alabama, the Equal Justice Initiative employed attorneys who found more cases of prisoners who had not received meaningful public defense. During this same time Alabama experienced tectonic shifts in its penitentiaries. Between 1990 and 2000, the state's prison population quadrupled. Violence behind bars began to rise. Food supplies and cleanliness reportedly plummeted.

One of the inmates who watched Alabama's prison landscape change was Junior Mack Kirby, perhaps a living embodiment of its incarceration boom. Kirby had two felony convictions for brewing vats of moonshine before picking up a third felony for burning down an empty tool shed. Prosecutors charged the shed incident as arson rather than vandalism. When Kirby was arrested again in 1990 for trafficking marijuana, he was sentenced to life in prison without the possibility of parole.

By 2000, the Alabama Legislature was forced to acknowledge just how many inmates were flooding into its prison facilities. Lawmakers amended Alabama's Habitual

Felony Offender Act to give trial judges more discretion in deciding which inmates were appropriate to be sentenced to life without parole. That cautious change in the law triggered dozens of letters arriving at the Equal Justice Initiative. One of the men who reached out was Junior Mack Kirby.

Stevenson remembers his first meeting with Kirby.

"He was someone who'd been working when he got arrested, but he still didn't make enough money to afford a good defense attorney," Stevenson recalls. "When he was sentenced to life, he didn't have money for the kind of lawyer who could have skillfully argued to a prosecutor about how these charges should be handled before the case went to trial—before it ever got as far as it did in the process. This happens a lot with clients we represent: Some are Vietnam vets with disabilities, some are drug addicts involved with minor incidents, some are homeless people. They don't have access to adequate defense when they first get into these situations. They are really quite vulnerable."

Stevenson has encountered inmates Alabama's HFOA law has sentenced to life for a fourth offense of writing a bad check or stealing a bicycle. In Junior Mack Kirby, Stevenson saw a man who had been sentenced to die in prison over moonshine, a shed fire and marijuana. The attorney believed it was a case he could win.

Even as the Equal Justice Initiative was challenging HFOA, it was also monitoring riots and dangerous living conditions in Alabama's prisons due to the influx of bodies. If voters thought attorneys in Stevenson's line of work were exaggerating the situation, by September of 2010 there were reasons for the public to think twice: In that month Alabama Chief Justice Sue Bell Cobb brought nearly all criminal judges from across the state to a meeting in Montgomery to discuss what she termed "a crisis" with prison overcrowding. Cobb pointed out during the three-day conference that Alabama's prisons were operating at one-hundred-and-ninety-five percent of their designated capacity. These concerns were reported by journalist Brian Lawson of *The Huntsville Times*, as was the Chief Justice's observation that the money Alabama spends on its prisons has quadrupled in the last twenty years. Lawson also interviewed Madison County criminal judge Karen Hall, who said her recent visits to the Elmore and Tutwiler correctional facilities startled her.

"I saw a hundred and ninety-five men in a dorm that was ninety-six degrees," Hall told *The Huntsville Times*. "They can go to church; they can play basketball or lift weights in their yard, and that's it. They need to be doing something."

Within two years of Judge Hall giving that interview, a major investigation by *The Birmingham News* revealed that between 2011 and 2012, inmate-on-inmate violence in Alabama prisons jumped by forty percent while assaults leading to serious injury nearly doubled: The findings were presented in an article by journalist Robin Demonia, who noted that inmate homicides were also up in 2012.

Alabama's rising prison violence did not go unnoticed by its state correctional officers. When the Southern Center for Human Rights filed a lawsuit against Donaldson Correctional Facility in Jefferson County, charging it was grossly under-reporting inmate-on-inmate violence, the Alabama Correctional Organization joined as a partner in the same legal action.

Public figures in Alabama began talking about California's new experiment, AB 109. Republican State Senator Cam

Ward, co-chair of Alabama's Senate Judiciary Committee, was among the first to mention the "realignment" happening on the West Coast. Ward had sponsored his own bill to make it difficult for county judges to sentence low-level thieves and simple drug offenders to lengthy prison terms. Ward is among a host of legislators no longer willing to ignore the price tag for Alabama's mass incarceration, now ringing in at more than $577 million annually. Moreover, Ward recognized the skyrocketing prison population might bring his state's correctional system down the path to a confrontation with the U.S. Supreme Court—the same path down which California has ventured.

"If we were to get sued and lose—and we would lose—a federal court could come in and take over our whole system," Ward told reporter Katherine Sayre of Mobile's *Press-Register*. "I don't think any of us want that."

The political mirrors between Alabama and California are fixed as much in the past as they are in the future: Both states have a history of "tough-on-crime" mandatory sentencing laws that operate without analytic flexibility. In 1994 California passed its "three-strikes" voter initiative. The measure came on the heels of a stomach-turning crime, in which 12-year-old Polly Klaas was kidnapped from her own bedroom by Richard Davis, a convicted abductor and brutal rapist. Klaas was sexually assaulted, murdered and left to rot under a board. During sentencing, Davis made lewd and disgusting remarks in the courtroom, displaying what many perceived to be a warped pride in the immeasurable agony he had inflicted on the Klaas family. In Richard Davis, Californians saw the lowest form of human life they could imagine. Voters wanted to prevent similar men from stalking their neighborhoods and passed the three-strikes measure, demanding any criminal defendant who'd already been convicted of two prior felonies be sentenced to twenty-five-years to life in prison if they were found guilty of a third.

California continues to produce criminals whom most agree should never have a chance of escaping genuine punishment due to a judge's fluke decision-making; however, the state's prisons are now overcrowded, unaffordable and officially illegal in the eyes of a federal court. In 2005, California's Legislative Analysis Office reported that the three-strikes law cost the state $500 million annually. California journalists are also aware of defendants serving extreme prison terms for minor crimes. These include inmates serving life for property crimes and drug activity. One case reporters honed in on was that of Leandro Andre, who—after racking up felony convictions for burglary and transporting marijuana—was sentenced to life in prison without parole for stealing VHS tapes from a Kmart.

Alabama's HFOA is a legal cousin of California's "three-strikes." HFOA mandates that any criminal defendant with three felony convictions be sentenced to life without parole when they commit a fourth class-A offense. Until HFOA's amendment in 2000, Alabama trial judges had no discretion in each case. According to the Alabama Sentencing Commission, before HFOA went into effect, the state's prisons held less than six thousand inmates. Twelve years later, in 1991, it had twenty-eight thousand men and women behind bars; and Junior Mack Kirby was one of them.

For Stevenson's part, he understands the thinking of American voters who support "three-strikes" for offenders who commit three violent crimes; but many cases of mandatory sentencing do not fit that mold: A large number involved stacks of non-violent transgressions.

"These laws are unfair because they treat all crimes equally when we know not all crimes have the same culpability and the same effects on public safety," Stevenson observes. "They are also incredibly expensive. To put a 25-year-old in prison for the next fifty years because he stole $100 is a very bad economic policy. There are better ways to punish offenders, and there are ways that are more effective and more cost effective. These laws are not really about public safety. They are about the politics of fear and anger, and more incarceration."

Junior Mack Kirby's case was glaring in Alabama because all of his HFOA convictions were nonviolent and three involved moonshine or marijuana.

"I don't think anything has contributed more to mass incarceration in the U.S. than the introduction of mandatory-minimum sentencing laws for drug offenders," Stevenson adds.

Kirby's case was brought back to the original trial judge who had sentenced him to life without parole. Despite the state's new amendment to HFOA, the judge declined to change Kirby's sentence. The Alabama Court of Criminal Appeals also ruled against Kirby's bid for another chance.

With Stevenson at his side, Kirby took his case all the way to the Alabama Supreme Court. In 2004, all nine justices agreed to overturn their lower courts. The highest legal body in the state deemed Kirby eligible for parole. The Alabama parole commission released him that same year, at the age of sixty-two.

It was a rewarding moment for Stevenson. "Mr. Kirby was overjoyed," the attorney recalls. "One of the greatest challenges for anyone who's been virtually sentenced to die in prison is that you're told there is no hope. It can become difficult for some inmates not to give in to hopelessness and end up doing destructive things. Mr. Kirby really avoided that. He never stopped trying to maintain hope."

STEVENSON STANDS AT the podium, looking out at the collection of judges from across Illinois. He brings them to the topic of mass incarceration in America. He moves through key points to contextualize the issue: In 1972 the U.S. had three-hundred-thousand people in jails or prison, while today that number is two-point-three million; there are now six million individuals on probation or parole; and one out of three black men between the ages of twenty and twenty-nine is in jail, prison, or on probation or parole. Just eight months before, Stevenson made the same observations to an audience in Long Beach, California, knowing that the Golden State continues to experience its own clashes over the effectiveness of mandatory sentencing laws. According to statistics from the Office of the Attorney General, California's crime rate dropped by fifty-percent between 1992 and 2011. Victims' advocates say mandatory sentencing played a key role in that decrease, keeping incorrigible offenders behind bars for longer spans of time. However, some legal analysts strongly disagree with a connection between California's increased public safety and its mandatory sentencing laws. Professor Robert Nash Parker, co-director of Presley Center for Crime and Justice at University California, Riverside, released a study in 2012 arguing the laws played virtually no role in the state's victories over crime. Parker contends California's falling arrest numbers correlate with a documented decline in alcohol consumption. Comparing California's crime rate with other highly populated states, such as Illinois and New York—states which don't have versions of "three-strikes"—the professor found crime rates dropped in similar ways. Parker also noted California's trend of falling crime began in 1992, two years before "three strikes" was passed.

When Stevenson spoke in Long Beach, he made a similar point about violent crime rates.

Now, facing the Illinois judges, he turns to a topic close to his heart, that of juveniles being treated as adult criminals. At 52-years-old, few images stand out in Stevenson's memory as much as a young adolescent he represented on a murder charge: He was a teen who'd watched his mother get beaten whenever her boyfriend came home drunk—a threat which happened enough to have already put her in the hospital twice. Making the situation worse was the fact that the boyfriend worked in law enforcement. The cycle of violence continued until one night the teenager watched his mother get knocked unconscious from a blow to her face. Stevenson's investigation into what happened next suggests that the boy—unable to revive his bleeding mother on the floor—momentarily believed she was dead. Walking into a bedroom, the teen ended the storm by killing his mother's abuser with the man's own pistol. Because the victim was a deputy sheriff, a judge certified the 14-year-old to stand trial as an adult. He would await his next court date in the county's adult jail facility. Stevenson became his lawyer three days later.

Stevenson paints a picture of his first meeting with the teenager for the Illinois judges. He recalls how his new client refused to speak for a long time and then broke down, convulsing and crying uncontrollably. Stevenson learned that for two nights in a row, the boy had been sexually assaulted in all manners, and forcibly raped, by a number of grown men inside the jail.

"When I left the courthouse I couldn't understand how this could happen," Stevenson says behind the podium. "Who did this? Well, we did this, by not thinking about the implications of what it means to be just, to be decent, to be fair…We're not helping those kids to recover. We're feeding that anger and frustration."

By the 1990s Stevenson had made ending the adult prosecution of juveniles one of his main missions. As the cases rolled on he continued to learn the horrors of putting teenagers in adult jail and prison facilities. Representing more and more clients in that situation, he has become convinced there is no place a teen is more vulnerable to physical and sexual violence than in an adult holding facility. The attorney has even found cases of defendants as young as twelve being put in such environments.

The Equal Justice Initiative kept challenging the adult prosecution of teenagers, especially in states across the South. Human Rights Watch and Juvenile Justice Project of Louisiana were also deep in the fight. In 2005, advocates won a major victory when the United States Supreme Court banned all judges from handing down the death penalty for juveniles. But even now twenty-nine states still permit the practice of holding juvenile offenders in adult facilities. The Equal Justice Initiative's most recent data indicates nearly ten thousand teenagers in America face this situation, either awaiting trial or after sentencing.

"It's pretty tragic," Stevenson explains when he talks to

journalists. "Kids are defined by their very capacity for change. The one thing we know about any juvenile we're looking at is that they will appear different, and talk different, and act different, in a few years. The healthier environment you put kids in, the better their chances will be. But the opposite is also true—put them in a dangerous, violent, destructive environment where there are no real caretakers, they'll become damaged—they won't develop into the kind of adult we want them to be. The way we've been handling it has created a legacy that's really quite troubling."

Even as Stevenson gives talks in states from California to Illinois, a number of civil rights attorneys have been settling a major lawsuit involving the intersection between teens and America's emerging private corporate prison industry. The lawsuit started two years earlier when attorney Robert B. McDuff joined forces with the Southern Poverty Law Center and American Civil Liberties Union to file a joint legal action on behalf of inmates at Walnut Grove Correctional Facility in Leake County, Mississippi. Walnut Grove prison is operated by GEO Group, the second largest for-profit prison company in the nation. Its inmates range in age from fifteen to twenty-two. Evidence filed in Mississippi court documents reports GEO Group was making $14 million per year from its contract to handle Walnut Grove prisoners.

An investigation by McDuff and his co-counsel paints a stark picture of the methods GEO Group used to convert its $14 million-a-year allotment for Walnut Grove into soaring profits, allegedly by keeping overhead low by dangerously understaffing its prison with questionable employees. The complaint filed in federal court against GEO Group states that in late 2010, a teen referred to as J.D. was placed in a new cell, prompting him to immediately raise concerns with a correctional captain that he was terrified of his cellmate. According to the lawsuit, that captain ignored J.D.'s fears. On January 22 of that year, J.D. sent a note to the unit manager of his prison wing "describing his fears and serious concerns for his safety." The next day, J.D.'s cellmate covered their cell door window with a towel and pulled out a makeshift knife. Holding the weapon to J.D., the cellmate sexually assaulted his teen victim. After the attacker went to sleep, J.D. wrote a note begging for help and then stood at his cell window, praying to glimpse a correctional officer.

"J.D. stood at the window for hours waiting for an officer to walk by or see him," the lawsuit states. "No officer came. The panic buttons in his cell did not work, so he had no way of obtaining help."

Like chronicling a bad dream, the legal action goes on to document that J.D.'s cellmate soon awoke, tied him to the bed with sheets and sexually tortured him for more than twenty-four hours. J.D. was also forced by his attacker to drink "blue cleaning liquid." The sun rose and set on the juvenile's episode of terror before a correctional officer realized what was happening.

Another incident in the lawsuit involved a unit manager at the prison intentionally labeling an inmate named Orlando Thomas "a snitch" to other prisoners on June 23, 2010. That same day Thomas was pummeled with brooms and food trays, kicked over and over and then stabbed with an ice pick.

Other allegations that were filed charged correctional officers and their superiors of being entirely complacent in

violent inmate-on-inmate attacks the staff knew were coming—
one of which occurred on February 27, 2010, leaving inmate
Michael McIntosh permanently brain damaged.

The lawsuit also included allegations that corrupt members
of GEO staff at Walnut Grove had sold drugs to prisoners under
their supervision, causing elevated violence in the facility, and
participated in the sexual exploitation of teens under their care,
triggering "significant" amounts of tension and violence in the
cell blocks. Many of these charges against GEO staff—along
with accusations of guard brutality—were later substantiated
by an independent investigation from the U.S. Department
of Justice. In a report issued by the federal investigators on
March 20, 2010, the Justice Department concluded that not
only was GEO staff at Walnut Creek indifferent to officer
brutality, inmate-on-inmate rape and staff sexually exploiting
teen prisoners, GEO was additionally "deliberately indifferent
to gang affiliations within the ranks of correctional staff."

In March of this year, Federal Judge Carleton Reeves held a
hearing in Southern Mississippi to make some determinations in
the civil action brought against Walnut Grove and GEO Group.
After reviewing evidence and testimony, Reeves signed a consent
decree against the private prison. The judge wrote in his ruling
that Walnut Grove "has allowed a cesspool of unconstitutional
and inhuman acts and conditions to germinate." Reeves added
that Mississippi correctional officials had been "derelict in their
duties" to monitor GEO Group and how it spent the taxpayer
money it received.

Walnut Grove is far from GEO Group's only prison facility.
It has bars for profit in Arizona, Florida, Texas and other states.
And GEO Group is not the only American corporation raking

in millions from the private incarceration boom. An ongoing series of investigations by *The Times-Picayune of New Orleans* this year determined more than half of Louisiana's inmates are being housed by private corporations. In a state with the highest incarceration rate in the U.S., one in seven of Louisiana's prisoners is housed by a single business, LaSalle Corrections. Reports from Cindy Chang of *The Times-Picayune* chronicle the methods LaSalle Corrections used to donate tens of thousands of dollars to political campaigns in Louisiana, infusing cash into the election coffers of county sheriffs, state lawmakers and Governor Bobby Jindal.

"With strategically placed contributions, they can influence legislation as well as potentially steer inmates to their own prisons," Chang wrote in one article. "Some of LaSalle Corrections' donations are to urban sheriffs who have a surplus of state-sentenced inmates and can choose where to send the overflow."

Louisiana officials may be relying on LaSalle, but GEO Group keeps a larger corporate presence in the American South and Midwest; and has accordingly spent hundreds of thousands of dollars with various county, state and national politicians from both parties. The mission is to ensure GEO continues to get contracts similar to what it had with the Walnut Grove Correctional Facility. Journalists working for *Reuters* and *The Palm Beach Post* found the paper trail for GEO's contributions to members of various state budget committees, who in turn have oversight of contracts with private prisons. GEO has also given tens of thousands of dollars—or more—to the American Legislative Exchange Council, which in the late 1990s coordinated an effort for states to pass versions of "three-strikes" and other mandatory minimum sentencing laws.

Concluding his remarks to the Illinois judges, Stevenson knows he is standing in one of the few states that has kept the private prison industry out of its jurisdictions. That was not true when Stevenson was giving his recent talk in California. In the midst of political fighting over the Realignment experiment, California lawmakers have begun contracting with none other than GEO Group, sending eight thousand of its overflow inmates to private prisons in Arizona, Oklahoma and Mississippi. It is a move toward a prison model Stevenson vehemently opposes. He is now representing a number of teenage inmates at Walnut Grove Correctional Facility, and the attorney knows how wrong the cash-for-prisoner compact can go when moved into the realm of Wall Street. Repeat offenders are returning customers.

"Private prisons are one of the worst developments in the last twenty-five years in terms of exploiting mass incarceration," Stevenson explains. "We now have people within an economic industry in this country who thrive on us having the highest prison population, and are happy about it. They live in a nation where not addressing criminal behavior, or mental illness, or the role of poverty in crime, are all economic wins for them. Innocent people going to prison is also an economic win for them...They are thrilled when the recidivism rates are the highest they've been."

So is there another vision? The massive flow of taxpayer dollars currently making businesses rich from perpetual crime could, in the view of Stevenson and other justice reformists, be used as major financial incentives for government-run jails and prisons to develop innovative drug treatment, behavioral rehabilitation, counseling services and job-training. But reformists are sure the only way to make that happen is to get Americans to balance their natural emotions around victimization with a logic that divorces the crime-hysteria that politicians count on to exploit.

Standing in front of the Illinois judges, it is hard for Stevenson to know how many of them believe in a different future; but the attorney who as a young man spent time with Rosa Parks continues to see a different path: He sees a nation where judges have more ability to consider the level of victimization when sentencing a defendant; a nation where teenage criminals are helped to develop rather than devolve; a nation where the calamity around crimes against the innocent and the disintegration of the offenders cannot be blatantly monetized to give CEOs and corporate shareholders a larger bonus. Like many of today's justice reformists, Stevenson is choosing to not give in to the culture of hysteria—but rather fight every day to replace it with a culture of problem-solving.

"It's very difficult for some people to care about the abuse of others, unless they fear that same abuse," Stevenson says when asked about his toughest challenges. "And right now the country is not having a holistic conversation. We need to be committed to preventing the conditions that are contributing to these crimes. Not talking about poverty when you're talking about crime is simply misguided. Not talking about a justice system that treats people better if they are already better off or wealthy is misguided. Not talking about our lack of access to mental health care is misguided. Not talking about the childhood trauma inflicted on those growing up in neighborhoods plagued by violence is misguided. This disconnect is undermining the discussion our nation really needs to have."

CHAPTER 5

June, Paloma, California: Apostle

CALAVERAS COUNTY SHERIFF'S Detective Josh Crabtree looks out his windshield at the wash of dimpled hills, an eddy of charred bronze sundering cattle range from open skies: Gypsum-light grass sweeps down to homes along the cottonwoods, and an isolated meth dwelling stands propped on a rent slope beyond their roofs. Crabtree's truck follows two unmarked SUVs and a sedan rolling down the gravel lane. A black car fills his rearview. "This guy is going to run or fight," Crabtree says, adjusting his sunglasses and checking ammunition clips fastened on the mesh Army vest over his Kevlar. "He always runs or fights."

The convoy passes a barn scrubbed in torn rails of paint. Weeds sway upward again. The bleached, green rods of a swing set flash by. The sedan accelerates, slashing banners of dust in the naked afternoon sun. The entire convoy aims at the beige house-shell hemmed in by garbage bags and colorless wash appliances. A battery of vehicle doors bang open. Crabtree swerves along a camper trailer, jumping out with his hand on his gun. Detective Tim Sterm, Deputy Alan Serpa and Parole Agent Diana Mauch cut through his peripheral vision, a blur of vests and badges along the old, oiled cords of a clothesline. It is so stifling it's hard to breathe. The detectives move by pepper-streaked planks of wood nailed to windows without glass. Crabtree and Parole Agent Romero clear the trailer. They cross a back incline, trotting up to an open sliding-glass door draped in a ripped bed sheet.

Crabtree notices a flick go shuddering through the blanket. His .40-caliber comes out. "Sheriff's department!" he yells. "Don't move." Romero covers him. The detective keeps his Glock on the sheet and uses his other hand to pull it back. In an instant the expression on Crabtree's face evaporates into the blaring heat. "Come on out, Roger," he says quietly. "Just get outside."

Roger "Country" Anderson emerges. Daylight skives his retinas. His teeth clench. A hard-carved uncertainly is twitching under his eyelids, bending the chafed, leathery tension in his face. "Hey, Josh," he manages as he glances up.

"Just sit there," Crabtree responds, peeling back the makeshift curtain again. "You get out here too, Lozano." The massive form of a man struggles through the sheet, taking a deep breath, dropping two-hundred-and-fifty pounds of girth onto a wobbly kitchen chair beneath the overhang.

Crabtree can hear the other officers confronting a group of individuals at the front of the house. He asks Lozano about the fugitive his team is searching for: "Is he in here or not?"

"He's not."

"Are you sure?

"Yeah."

The detective stares back at the fouled sheet. "Can I go in and look?"

Gabriel Lozano exhales. "If you want."

Crabtree signals Romero and ducks through the portal.

The man called "Country" leans back limp in his jeans and weathered shirt. He shuts his eyes from the blowing warmth. "Hi, Roger," a soft voice drifts over him. Country binds his brow. His eyes fight open again. Diana Mauch, his former parole agent, is standing there. She's calm in her dark glasses, designer denim and Kevlar vest. Roger feels sweat needling from his brown shock of hair down to the sandy shadow of whiskers on his jaw line. He pushes the word "hey" through a dryness in his throat. Mauch studies his weight loss, seeing how his features have been drilled skullish, with tightening grooves and canyonous tissue gaps eroding into face-bone. Mauch looks down at him. The ex-con glances south to the barren tides of grass—a rolling span of fried, suede desolation. He gets lost in the emptiness, watching the crisp, wild oats tremble to foam in the bending sunrays.

Roger Anderson. Age: Fifty-two. Vocational skills: Gas and electric worker, journeyman carpenter, certified welder. Talents: Woodworking, guitar playing, singing gospel and country music. Tested I.Q.— one hundred and twenty-three. Total time spent in California state incarceration: twenty-one years. In western Calaveras, he's "Rog" or "Country," a U.S. Army platoon leader who came home from Korea in 1977 to find his favorite uncle slamming proponone-derived methamphetamine—biker crank—in an empty bathroom one night. Roger offered his own muscular arm to the needle, reaching out for three decades of unholy matrimony. His first few years existing as a meth fiend were tedious: Telling lies to foremen; stealing from family members; dropping jobs in San Francisco; telling bosses he had an allergy to kumquats to explain the bleeding craters he was picking in his face. One night in the city's Tenderloin district he dug a dime-size hole in his back with a curtain hanger.

Roger finally crossed the line on November 11, 1984, when he wandered into a 7-Eleven convenience store in Santa Rosa, California. All he wanted was chocolate milk and a carton of cigarettes. He found them. He bought them. He headed out. It wasn't until Roger was halfway through the swing doors that it occurred to him the female store attendant was entirely alone. Vaulting over the counter, he showed her a knife, robbed the register and then jumped back over to leave a clear palm print for detectives to track.

Booked into Deuel Vocational Institution for armed robbery, Roger earned the nickname that stayed with him for life. His cellmate was trying to sing a tune. Roger sat back and listened. His earliest memories were tangled in the songs of George Jones, jukeboxes lit by the soothing huskiness in "The Possum's" voice, how it carried the feeling of a long, bright sunset, the throat punished by cigarettes and whisky summoning notes that rang as a wounded harp, channeling neon hues of doubt and regret. Roger modeled his singing style after Jones, and, like his hero, its velvet torment was intrinsically linked to battling the demon of amphetamines. When Roger's celly started with the sour notes, Roger jumped in, his own voice a dark honky-tonk landscape of sound echoing through the perfect acoustics of DVI's hallways. Inmates down the row started applauding. After that, on most nights when the lights went out on Roger's block, his fellow convicts would call out, "Hey Country, sing us one!"

Roger was transferred from DVI to San Quentin Prison. When he was released two years later, he had tattooed visages of Doc Holiday, John Wayne and The Outlaw Josie Wales punched onto his back under the western ink banner, Stone Cold Country. The words were a tribute to George Jones, whose songs of pain incarnate kept playing like broken records in Roger's thoughts—those deep, soulful echoes of contagious self-punishment. "Hell Stays Open All Night Long."

Freedom did not keep Roger away from late night "water" rendezvous: By 1991 his meth use had sent him to Corcoran prison, where he spent a year in the B yard for violent offenders.

His next stint beyond stonewalls lasted five years. In 1996, parole violations connected to a burglary brought Roger to the gates of Old Folsom Prison. After being released he went back to Santa Rosa and tried to settle into family life with a wife, three sons and daughter.

The world went to flames on July 5, 1998.

His eyelids and neurotransmitters were blinking together. Sirens were wailing. A fog of chemical stimulus, cell death and axon decay were rolling hard on his senses, but his heart rate slowed just enough to realize he was leading a vehicle pursuit with the Sonoma County Sheriff's Department. A moment of crystallized horror took hold as Roger saw the blue police lights flashing over his 3-year-old son in the back seat. Roger thought his wife had taken the infant out of the truck before he fled the house. Now he kept his foot on the accelerator, trying to make it to his sister's address. His plan was to hand the child to his sister at the door and then slit his own throat with his Jim Bowie knife. Roger was convinced the car chase would earn him his "third strike" under the law, along with a life sentence in prison. There would only be a few seconds when the truck stopped. Bolting onto his sister's porch, he found the front door locked as three sheriff's deputies drew down on him with their pistols. Roger put his son on the far right of the porch and then moved, guiding the gun barrels with him. In one motion he pulled his Bowie knife and slit his own throat. He threw the knife down. Blood poured and spouted. Roger's body made an unexpected movement. The deputies opened fire on him.

Country's next flash of vision was a paramedic over him, yelling for plasma. His eyes opened: His throat was nearly cut to the jugular and there were bullet holes in his hip and leg.

A newspaper photographer videotaped the standoff, an action that likely saved Roger from spending his natural life in prison. The footage convinced a judge to drop the hostage charge against him. A number of other counts, including felony evading, would stand. Roger was processed in to Pleasant Valley State Penitentiary in Coalinga in 1998. He was looking at an eleven-year term. Country was eventually transferred back to Old Folsom Prison.

These were the dark, endless hours that came to define Roger's existence. These were silent moments when he was overtaken by visions of bullets meant for him going into the skull of his little son, or his sister's child, who had been behind the door in the line of fire just minutes before the guns opened up. Even though no one else was shot, dead little ones swam through his Circadian rhythms. The images would flame up as a gagging repulsion moved like a rod down his throat. He'd go into uncontrollable fits of tears. An actualized memory reeled him back, further in time, deeper into the emotional filth, opening his mind up to the trauma he had caused the clerk he'd robbed at knifepoint, and the nightmares—the psychic trauma— she would likely endure for the rest of her life. His thoughts were roaring with unholy lucidity. Now Roger felt his victim's sick, acute terror curling under his own ribs. When he processed his actions through the values he'd been taught by his parents, Martin and Mary, his consciousness clotted into blinding pain.

Martin and Mary would embark on half-day treks to visit, inspiring him to describe his parents to other inmates as the most giving people he had ever known. Roger was contemplating if there was still a way to make them proud.

"I learned a lot from my folks," he would attest. "They've always been responsible. Never missed a bill. Never let a person down. My dad, he would go without to do for someone else— that's the kind of man my father is."

A visit from Mary toward the end of Roger's term at Folsom triggered an epiphany about the politics of the yard. He had been acting as a "key holder" or "shot caller" for the white inmate groups. He was wielding influence. Roger's mom had driven more than four hours to see him; yet drama circulating from cellblocks to the fence lines was consuming his thoughts. He couldn't even concentrate on enjoying his mother's visit. Roger decided he was done with the yard. When he left the gates on May 30, 2007, his addiction to meth hadn't disappeared but his tolerance for the criminal lifestyle had.

Roger was arrested by the Calaveras County Sheriff's Department in June of 2009 for being under the influence of methamphetamine. Three months later, he checked himself into the adult program of Sacramento Valley Teen Challenge. He excelled in the new environment, eventually getting appointed the lead male singer in a choir made up entirely of women from crisis centers in Lincoln and Yuba City. After he graduated, he wasn't going anywhere. Every Sunday for nearly two years he continued to sing with the choir.

"At his own cost, almost on a weekly basis, he travels with our choir, helping raise funds and to spread a message of hope for those with life-controlling issues," the program manager wrote of Roger to a Calaveras County judge. The man called Country would remember those choir dates as the best times in his life. In 2010, after a stint in rehab, Roger stood in a tuxedo in front of a huge crowd in Sacramento and brought his 7-year-old granddaughter on stage. "Because of my drug use, this is the first time I've seen her in two years," he told the audience, fighting back tears. "It's because of forgiveness that I can spend tonight with this beautiful girl and my daughter." Roger then lifted his microphone and launched into the gospel piece "Forgiven Again." His voice forced its way up to the chandeliers, a soaring baritone survivor, a refrain of weathered grace powered by raw emotion.

But Country's role in the spiritual revival came with a cost. Traveling from town to town, he came to know the recovering female addicts in the choir. Their stories of childhood trauma penetrated him. He learned that every one of them had been molested as a child or raped as a young lady. Roger began to understand there was a searing scar tissue around their core, an organ-liner of sheer pain that made addiction feel like a waiting angel of comfort. Tall and muscular, Roger put on a brave face when hearing the girls' stories, only to be overcome by tears in private moments. One Sunday he watched an abuse survivor share her tale with an entire congregation about being raped multiple times as a child by someone she knew. When the church service was over, Roger wiped his eyes and quietly took her aside.

"Where can I find that man," he demanded. "Let me know where this guy is, because I'll handle it. I'm serious."

The girl just smiled.

But Roger was earnest. Months before, he'd become friends with a young mother of three children. The woman came to trust him enough to share that she's just discovered her skinhead boyfriend—the same man who had blackened her eye and broken her ribs—had also molested her 8-year-old daughter. She was finally ready to escape the psychopath but he was still coming around the house, trying to see her, trying to force his control. Roger investigated the situation by talking to the family's neighbors: They told him "a lot of bad things" were going on at the house, though they didn't want to get involved themselves. "You're just like all the guys in the Pen," Roger snapped with disgust. "You talk and talk, but when rubber meets the road, you aaaiiin't gonna bust a grape. Guess it's up to the old guy to do something."

Roger called the neo-Nazi on the phone. "You need to come out and meet me," he challenged. "Step up and meet me like a man, because I will bury you. I'll bury you for good."

The skinhead hung up and moved out of the state the following week, never contacting his victims again.

Roger's rage at men who hurt women soon towed him back into the orbit of violence. On April 2, 2011, he heard a close female friend had been battered in a confrontation with her boyfriend. Roger's psyche was already scaling a meth-mounted plateau, his senses rousing in a hard neurotoxin Nirvana. He raced to the boyfriend's house in his truck, stepping out and grabbing a heavy oak branch carved like a baseball bat. Roger's plan was to straighten out the man who'd hurt his friend; yet he was so high on meth that he attacked the boyfriend's cousin. Roger took one full swing with the weapon—blasting his target full in the face—before he realized the wrong man was crumpling to the ground.

Roger was charged with felony assault. He was facing state prison time again. Ultimately, letters of support from churchgoers and treatment counselors convinced a judge to drop the crime to a misdemeanor. He was sentenced to a year on an ankle bracelet.

The next year Roger was singing every Sunday at a church in Burson. It was during this period he started building toys for children who had lived in violent households. Time went by with the calm motions of constructing an intricate, hand-made doll cradle for one girl and a flashy World War I biplane for her cousin. Roger had also met a woman in the county's Courage to Change program with a young son recovering from family chaos. He built the boy a flatbed diesel truck that verged on being a work of art.

Now, Roger watches law enforcement swarm the house in Paloma. He thinks about his own yard and the series of decorative birdhouses he's been working on for a woman who has adopted five "drug babies." If Roger had just stayed home today he would still be crafting those birdhouses—he would still be engaged in the sort of task that had built his rapport with Detective Crabtree. On the face of it, the two men have an unlikely connection: One an accomplished investigator and decorated SWAT member, and one a neck-tatted parolee with a rap sheet the size of the Dead Sea Scrolls. But Crabtree has come to appreciate Roger's piercing insights into the world of methamphetamine, as well as his absolute refusal to make excuses for the torrents of pain, tragedy and communal destruction it fans through his jurisdiction; and though

Roger often falls and fails, the ex-convict continues to dream of being a man who makes positive contributions to the little ranching county he's come to love. And for Crabtree, after years of staring through a dirty and ever-moving menagerie of homicides, assaults, armed robberies and child abuse cases, he has to hope that Roger "Country" Anderson could be a kind of apostle to the droves of meth addicts who are changing the soul of the central Gold Country. Crabtree is too cerebral of a detective—too cerebral of a man—to hope for less while passing through this shadow-line in his career. Josh Crabtree and Roger Anderson are veterans who've been edging along the same psychological precipice: They have a shared, unspoken empathy for the highs and lows that come with gazing down into the predatory abyss. And so whom else could any cop turn to for a sliver of hope? If Roger Anderson, twice-shot, neck-slit, and fatally overdosed, can walk out of the lifestyle, then maybe willpower can stand up against the bleak inevitability spreading from the drug.

Crabtree is not the only law enforcement officer showing confidence in Roger. Diana Mauch, his former parole agent, has been so impressed by Roger's desire to break the area's cycles of addiction and crime that she's been preparing to bring him to local schools as an expert speaker on the dangers of drug use. Roger would do anything to help "sweet Diana." He met her under embarrassing circumstances, but strove to do good for her while on parole. Later, when singing on tour with the choir, the group stopped at Mauch's church for a performance. Roger would never forget working his voice into the spirit, and looking out at the pews to see Mauch smiling back at him.

CRABTREE AND ROMERO emerge from the hanging sheet over the sliding glass door.

"Get up and turn around," Crabtree orders.

Roger pauses. The mends of sleepless flesh around his orbitals wrench into an agonized hook. "What?" he stutters, "Wha—what is it?"

"You know," Crabtree says, "I've probably never felt this bad about arresting someone before." The words slip through a half-conscious, pressurized breath. "I can honestly tell you I wish I didn't come to work today."

Roger feels the handcuffs speed down on him. "Man, I'm just here to have a mountain bike photographed for eBay," he offers. "I don't know about any of this; I ain't mixed in it."

Crabtree keeps his eyes down, locking the cuffs: "I'm sorry, you're going."

"Why?"

"You don't know why?"

"Josh, I don't."

Crabtree shakes his head and looks away.

Roger begins to plead: "C-Come on, at least tell me why I'm going to jail?"

The detective halts. "You really don't know why?" he asks, muted. Before Roger can answer Crabtree takes his arm, pulling the corpse-waif away from Lozano and out into the warmth and irradiated grass. "Come here and we'll talk about why," Crabtree says. "You're going because there's a ton of meth in that house, packaged for sales, and you were sitting right next to it."

"Are you serious?"

"Don't Roger. Just don't."

"They told me they were just doing eBay."

"It's all right there on the table."

"But they—" Roger senses the strength ebb from his lungs. Panting, he stares down at the black rot eating at the camper's window covers. He can hear three of his acquaintances being taken into custody in the front yard. "I just had this bike," Roger mumbles.

Crabtree looks back at the greasy layer over the door. "This is a sales operation; and it looks like there's stolen equipment all over the place." The veteran cop is thinking aloud in a tense, absent tone. "And I can't believe I just found you, of all people, right in the middle of it. This is probably one of the worst days I've had on the job in years—finding you in this house."

Roger's brow clamps into hard, sun-scorched furls, wet and reddening. "Please don't arrest me."

"Do you have any idea how many residents have been burglarized lately? Do you have any clue how out of control it's been in Valley Springs?"

"But I ain't part of all that."

"You were inside the house, with everything I just saw."

"Yeah, but—"

"I can't do anything: You're going."

"Josh, man, I—"

Crabtree pivots away. Glancing at Diana Mauch, the detective mumbles, "I seriously can not believe this."

"It's sad," Mauch agrees, stepping closer to her former parolee. "Roger, I was going to bring you to that conference to speak to all those kids." She lifts her eyebrows. "That's all over now."

Roger can hear the other addicts near the front getting

called in on their warrants. His chin guides back to the officers. His irises are deadening. "You know I don't do this."

Mauch slips her sunglasses off. "Then why are you here, Roger?" The soft phrase settles over him. "Listen," Mauch observes, "When you're clean, and when you're trying to do good, you do really good. You're one of the best. So don't tell me that when you rolled up here today you were confused. Roger, you know better than anyone what this place is. And you knew it when you pulled up."

Worn muscles in the addict's starved neck calm their creasing. Petrified sweat beads ride his labored breaths. "Yeah," he whispers. "Yeah, I knew."

"I've got to search you," Mauch says.

Roger brings his eyes up to meet her: "Be careful. It's in my left sock above my shoe."

"What?"

"A needle."

"You're all the way back to needles?"

"Yeah, but I don't know why I brought it."

Mauch pulls the ex-con's pant leg up to find a hypodermic rig fastened below his calf with medical tape. Roger musters a look at Crabtree. "I tried to call you last week, Josh."

The detective glances back. "I know," he answers quietly. "I wasn't putting you off. I was just buried with work. I was just…."

"—I tried, man, I tried," Roger goes on. "I wanted to tell you I was fucking up. You know I don't want this."

Crabtree guards his expression behind the black blades of his glasses.

"But Josh," Roger continues, "I swear, I haven't been

stealing from nobody. I ain't even with these people, you know. I'm just using. I'm not hittin' houses or helping anyone hit houses. Shit, you know I don't ever do that. Two things I've always hated: Thieves and cranksters, even though I've been both in my life."

"I believe you don't want to hurt other people."

"Just me—I keep all this on myself."

Crabtree clears his throat: "So, you don't think anyone else coming through this place is hurting people?"

"You're right, I shouldn't have been here."

"So why did you do it?" Mauch interrupts. "You were doing so well, and for so long."

Roger's bleached bottom eyelids wilt down. "The loneliness got me this time," he admits.

"God Roger, this is going to break your mother's heart," Mauch utters.

"Don't tell her."

The parole agent shakes her head. "I'm not going to call her," she assures him. "But you're not dumb. You're anything but dumb. You know this is a small town. The neighbors are already outside watching, looking at these patrol cars and people in handcuffs. And here you are, Roger. You don't think your parents are going to hear about what happened today?"

Chest heaving, Roger responds, "You're right, they're gonna know."

"Listen," Crabtree says, "don't go thinking the world is over. You'll get through this."

Roger hears the coarseness easing out of the detective's voice in a way that hints to the confidence they once shared. The ex-convict's face stiffens into a tortured totem of gradual recognition. His eyes tear up as they move over the scalded grass of the hillsides. "Shit, why did I do this," he huffs. "I just can't be by myself. It wasn't too bad when I was living with my parents. But then I moved out on my own, and it was the loneliness this time. Had no one to talk to. The loneliness was crushing me. I just woke up one time at two in the morning and said, 'I can't take it, I can't—I've got to get high.'"

Calaveras County Sheriff's Detective Josh Shemenski pulls in. He has just come from arresting one of the King brothers in Valley Springs. The King boys hold a secure place in Shemenski's consciousness: He hooked both of them last year for robbing their own grandmother. The confessions Shemenski got from the brothers read like bad fiction in his report. They descended on the elderly woman in her sleep, aggressively wrestling the purse from her fragile, fighting arms. After batting the purse from their grandmother's grasp, they took her last $70 in cash to buy methamphetamine. Shemenski's investigation earned one brother prison and the other probation. Now, finding the younger half of the duo high on meth this morning, Shemenski took it as a bad omen for Valley Springs. The ink on the booking documents was barely dry when Shemenski got the call to come to the house in Paloma. He climbs out of his car, noticing four men and a woman detained by officers in the driveway. Down along the trees he spots Roger Anderson and Gabriel Lozano in handcuffs near the side patio.

Shemenski peers through an open door into the house. Frayed wires snake from walls and hang in knots from spore-traced ceilings. A black silt of runny, half-boiled clay is festering along the floorboards. The waft of fecal mist hits his senses, lingering long and stale in the air. It will be two hours before

Shemenski's partner arrives with a search warrant for the house. When the two of them finally walk inside, they'll discover piles of garbage on the carpet, what appear to be a dozen stolen chainsaws and forty grams of methamphetamine between a table and an icebox. They'll also find a charred, dead rat inside the microwave oven, along with a bag of popcorn.

For now Shemenski wanders over to talk to Crabtree and Mauch. He lifts the navy-blue bill of his ball cap to see Roger Anderson trembling. Shemenski looks at him. The narcotics agent has a careful, contemplative stare that seems to put the most erratic dope fiends at ease. It is a gaze that shows serious inquiry over a rush to judge, and there are few meth or heroin users that don't take from it a confidence to tell a piece of the truth. Shemenski is also known on the streets as the detective who, though he doesn't smoke himself, always has a cigarette ready to hand to cooperative arrestees before the handcuffs speed down. But at this moment Shemenski's calm demeanor does little for Roger Anderson.

"I just don't want to go," Roger pants.

"You probably won't even be in there two days," Crabtree responds. "The way things have been lately."

"I've already been in there twenty-four years. I can't do a couple days."

Crabtree rubs his temple. "Roger, look around," he blurts, pointing to Detective Sterm and Detective Poortinga loading people into patrol cars. "Do you see what's happening here? This isn't about whether I like you." Crabtree pauses, easing off a tired breath. "Come on, Roger, you're going."

The ex-convict nods. He glances one last time at Mauch, lifting his emaciated frame forward.

"I almost feel sick to my stomach," Crabtree offers quietly before double-checking the steel bracelets cutting into the man called Country.

TWO DAYS LATER, Roger Anderson is granted an ordered release from jail. He drops into his car and careens into memories of the last year. The ankle bracelet he'd been forced to wear for his baseball bat assault came off on December 5, 2011. Roger started jabbing a needle in his arm the next day. He would feel the stimulant course through his blood, decimating the loneliness that breathed through his flashbacks. After thirty years of having methamphetamine crawl under his skin, Roger knew if he had the drug he would never be alone. There would always be men at his side professing friendship. There would always be women offering sex and emotional support. When the bracelet came off Roger understood that meth could build a familiar fortress around him. And it did—though now that fortress was collapsing faster than ever.

The insanity started escalating when his best friend, James Livezey, got arrested for killing Marvin Brown. Livezey was one of three people in the world Roger would have taken a bullet to protect. The headlines around the slaying—the testimony of Kevin Patton—had transmuted for Roger to something like a foreign language. "Jimmy never went over there to kill him," Roger had insisted to his parents. "That man would give anyone the shirt off his back. Besides, he ain't even the one who set off the whole chain of events." Opinions aside, whenever Roger thinks of the bulbous tumor slowly killing Livezey inside county jail the force of that dark evening in the Sequoia Rose Mobile Home Park steams through his equilibrium.

Driving through the open countryside, images of Livezey's impending death fade behind a more immediate and inescapable pain: Billy.

Billy was Roger's other best friend. On a dark night in Stockton, Roger had taken the unusual risk of giving himself a "speed ball" injection of meth combined with heroin. He and Billy were sitting in an empty parking lot when Roger's heart went into cardiac arrest. The man called Country was dying again. But Billy would not let it happen: He fought the overdose with all his energy, frantically doing CPR on Roger until paramedics arrived. Medical responders eventually told Roger that Billy had made all the difference. Nevertheless, Roger would not be present on April 13, 2012, when Billy himself died of a methadone overdose in Modesto, California. Now, Roger cannot escape the picture of Billy passing from the world, utterly alone on a dirty, anonymous floor. Worse yet, a funeral home burned Billy into ashes and then locked his remains away after no family members surfaced to pay the cremation fee. For six months Roger has been trying to save the money to liberate Billy's remnants from the morgue. In the meantime, he keeps with him Billy's most prized possession, a painting by Billy's mother, and guards it with his life.

Roger keeps driving. The words of Crabtree and Mauch are still with him. For Roger, these honest, hardworking professionals reflect all the best traits of his parents, whom the addict knows will soon learn of his latest arrest in Paloma. The episode means Martin and Mary Anderson, along with Roger's church congregation, will again face the prospect of whether methamphetamine is drilling Calaveras's future emptier than the mineshafts under its soil. On the larger scale, Roger knows he'll forge another link in a seemingly endless chain of statistics, especially one Solomon Moore just reported in *The New York Times*, which shows two-thirds of ex-convicts return to prison within three years of being released. Months later, when told about AB 109 and California's Realignment, Roger will feel only a perplexed curiosity about the mechanics of the law. He's sure no longtime outlaw would choose spending an extended term in the small, concrete dimensions of a county jail over a state prison, with its gyms, grassy yards, open skies, hotplates, personal televisions and school classes. He also understands a more immediate reality of letting the entire meth world know the vast majority of the crimes they commit against others will net little more than short stops at county jail—where dire overcrowding will force early release— a development bound to send the message there are few consequences to their sporadic rampages.

Roger can endlessly analyze failures within drug treatment and criminal reprogramming, though for him the dysfunction ultimately bottoms out in a crater of excuses. He believes he's always had control. He chooses to stick a needle in his arm every day, just as he chooses to never put a needle in anyone else's. He chooses to tell the truth about his time in prison, while he also chooses to never romanticize those days to younger addicts. He chooses to spend time with people he knows steal, and he occasionally chooses to confront them about the sense of violation they delve out. Roger often thinks of a meth-addicted mom he once chose to be friends with; and then how he'd chosen to kick in a bedroom door one night, roaring about the needles her friend left on the floor where her children could step on them.

He can still picture the door panel whacking open as the mom shrieked, "Why did you do that?"

"Same reason the cops do!" Roger yelled back, a rough creak spindling through his drawl, "Because it's disss-orrr-ieee-nting!"

Enough hurting innocents, Roger tells himself, and enough making excuses. He is convinced addicts have control. He has always had the control; and so he accepts that he's done all of this to himself.

Driving along the hills of Jenny Lind, it dawns on Roger that fines from his new arrest will make it impossible to claim Billy's ashes. Reality floods the foreground: Where the outlaw once ducked from horrid, racking visions, he now sees coffin-clutched friends that are, or soon will be. As much as any point in his painful and pain-inflicting existence, Roger Anderson is crushingly tired of breathing.

His bony hands keep to the steering wheel. Pitch-dark silhouettes brush telephone poles and broken gravel berms along O'Rielly Street. The path makes a steep descent into an open country view. There, at the end, Roger makes out an oak tree lifting off the bent, dry weeds. He aims his car directly at it, pounding the accelerator. The road comes rushing in—and the world disassembles into a cacophony of steel-spit glass.

Three days go by. Roger approaches the detectives' office for the Calaveras County Sheriff's Department. His scratches and bruises are hidden with sunglasses and an old hat over a bandana. He is not sure what he wants to say to Crabtree. These encounters are never easy. After Billy's death, one of Roger's favorite treatment counselors had been ready to quit. The cycles of hurt and loss were too overwhelming. Roger found the counselor at her office and threw his arms around her.

"You can't quit," he had insisted. "You're only seeing what goes wrong and the people who don't make it; but you've helped more people than you'll ever know. And not everybody can do your job—can handle what you can handle. And if you give up, how are the rest of us around here going to find the strength to not give up on each other?"

Roger was not sure his words had gotten through. But how could he find a language that channeled all the unknown truths from his side of the needle? How could he really communicate the self-destructive state of mind that convicts have when they're not high? Or the constant fear of living? Or how in prison you have to be strong, even hard, to survive; but on the outside asking others for help feels like the same weakness that makes you a target behind the walls? He had not found everything he wanted to say to the counselor. Now, walking into Crabtree's office, he is again searching for the words.

"How's it going?" the detective asks.

"I'm kind of laying low," Roger admits. "Listen, I'm sorry for putting you in that position."

"You know, a lot of people believed in you," Crabtree reflects. "I've been doing this for a long time, and for me and some of my partners, seeing an addict do what you were trying to do is the light at the end of the tunnel." He pauses for an instant and then adds, "Personally, I don't expect someone like you—who's done what you've done and survived what you survived—not to have some relapses."

Tears well up in Roger's eyes.

"Think about your life," Crabtree says. "You've been shot; your neck has been cut, you've o.d.'d numerous times. Roger, you should be dead. Maybe there's a reason you're not. Listen, because of everything you've done, you could influence these addicts in a way we could never hope to influence them. You know how to talk to people. You've got charisma. I still think you could make more of a change around here than you ever realized."

Roger huffs against bridling emotions.

"But," the detective continues, "what just happened to you happened because you were trying to save people by yourself."

Roger nods.

"You've got to quit trying to do it that way," Crabtree adds.

Taking a breath, Roger looks up: "Yeah, that's true."

And before Roger Anderson exits the office, he knows the journey will go on. More nights with the needle are ahead; more days of inspiring confidence in people only to let them down; more sleepless spells of self-loathing. And there will be more moments of weighing the question that consumes the deepest recess of his thoughts. Why does he keep craving methamphetamine? Why does he keep enabling a criminal culture that victimizes his own community?

"It's not the wire, it's the rush," Roger always says. "It's not a fucking disease, it's a fucking choice. I choose to do it. The one question I've never been able to answer is why."

YEAR II

"He felt warm and sticky from the bleeding.
Each time he felt the horn coming. Sometimes
the bull only bumped him with his head. Once
the horn went all the way through him and he
felt it go into the sand. Some one had
the bull by the tail."

Ernest Hemingway *In Our Time*

CHAPTER 6

Hell under the hardbreds

CONNER WOOD YANKS his helmet off, a breeze slipping by him to the iron line of bull chutes. Horns, muscle and hide idle as caged units of quiescent fury; and above, twenty-four inmates of Angola Prison can hear those nostrils snorting and the ton-laden hooves weighing down the dirt. Conner hunches a little. He knows how he looks to the crowd, a chess piece on the bleacher board of convicts divided from the throngs by an aviary of chain-link diamonds. Each rider waits in the sun. A few stare from canvas fishing hats while others hold tall in their light straw Stetsons. From a distance the figures are softened by their western shirts—the long black-and-white stripes of the condemned.

A bearish moan comes huffing from the earth-speckled toro in the first cell. Its hindquarters knock metal. A grey crust is caked to its mouth. Such four-legged combatants trace origin to Sonny Lewis and Bubba Dunn, well-known stock contractors just north in Alexandria: There's no mercy in them. Only a few bars separate the inmates from these horn-heads bred for blood, and across the way a multicolored stadium is filled with twelve thousand eager Louisianans.

The spring brightness moves on the river stone shape of Conner's head. Rangy cheeks, spotless skin, the sunrays only darken the chin stubble on his drawn, colorless features. He's not hot. It's the coolest April Saturday on record in this region of the South. Connor's been running and lifting weights to prepare for what is ahead. Last year was his first taste of rodeo action. He came out in two riding events. Now he has a want for it.

A lone reporter makes his way into the fenced bleachers of inmates.

"Bulls?" the stranger asks before sitting down.

"Yeah," Conner answers, a soft stroke of the eastern parishes brushed through his voice.

"Ever been injured?"

"I got kicked in one of my bones last year," he replies in barely more than a whisper, "but I wasn't hurt too bad. "

"Why are you out here?"

Shrugging, Conner responds, "It's just the thrill." His eyes move out to a line of flags being galloped in for the grand entrance. "Just," his voice tries to pick up, "just something to finally break the monotony."

The journalist nods. "So breaking that is worth the chance of getting hurt?"

"Well, I'm a little nervous now; but when that chute opens, I'm not going to be too scared."

"How old are you?"

Conner's hand moves over the porcelain sheen of his head: "I'm twenty-one."

"Do you mind me asking how long that monotony lasts?"

Fine, thin eyebrows lift on the young brow, his throat

working the words against a sudden dryness. "Oh, I'm—I'm in for life," he offers with a polite stutter. "I caught my charge when I was fifteen years old."

The other nods.

Conner hears his name called. He shakes hands with the journalist. Pushing his helmet back on, he lopes his lean frame down the narrow row of chutes. He stops at his pen. Inside, a light, flat-horned hammerhead is taking deep breaths. Fine wisps of hair hang down its ears. Cowhands help Conner and a platoon of other inmates onto their animals. The Angola Prison Rodeo has to start with a maelstrom, and so the opening event is Bust Out, which the penitentiary bills as sending "eight large, angry bulls" into the arena at once while eight "convict cowboys" test their grit by trying to stay on. The announcer's voice comes flaring through the speakers. Conner turns his hand through a dull knot of rope battening him down to his adversary. The noise of the crowd simmers in a tighter hum, playing over the whirled webs of razor and shiny green fields to the west.

Eight chute doors bang open in a salvo of metallic snaps. The granite-shouldered cluster of instinct beneath Conner plows forward, hunching, diving and crashing into the red, white and blue panel of the lower gate. The concussive jab turns the guts under Conner's legs, and he can sense his own spine drilling down into a mirage of hooves and flying dirt fragments.

It is over.

Conner looks up at streamers running across the awnings— pigmy flares of ruby, blue and cotton shark teeth swiveling against the crystal sea-shield of the sky.

Blood. Three inert bodies. He left no one breathing in the

house on Shady Lane: The newspaper called it "a scene of carnage."

Conner Wood grew up in Concordia Parish, a land of televangelists and Delta Bluesmen a hundred miles up the Mississippi River from Angola. Conner was not old enough to have a driver's license on the dark morning when he walked into his parents' bedroom, holding one of their guns, and executed both while they slept. It was 2 a.m. Conner's 16-year-old friend Matthew Whittington was present during the slayings. Whether or not Whittington helped plan the shootings remains an emotional point of debate in the town of Ferriday. What is known is that shortly after John and Geraldine Wood were permanently ended, Conner turned on Whittington, using a different gun kept in the house to drill nine bullets into his teenage neighbor. He was arrested that morning and charged with triple homicide. He reportedly told a Concordia Parish Sheriff's detective he had grown tired of his parents constantly fighting and wanted to silence the chaos.

Conner eventually pleaded not guilty by reason of insanity. When two psychiatrists declared the 15-year-old competent to stand trial his attorneys altered the plea to a standard "not guilty." Journalists from *The Concordia Sentinel* did what they could to describe the "baby-faced" defendant inside the courthouse. It was a challenge for any writer to capture how he looked on the witness stand, seated behind a microphone that dwarfed the length of his jaw, with his brown, deep-set child eyes looking away, an unkempt fuzziness along the top of his military buzz cut, a thread of tension in his small lips, his lace-light complexion nearly matching his pressed cotton shirt.

Conner was sentenced to three consecutive life terms. He was transferred to the David Wade Correctional Center, a special protection facility that would hold him until he became a legal adult and lifetime resident of Angola Prison.

Now Connor lies in the dust. Whooping acclamations ring through the air. He lifts himself up. The eight-way bull-run left every convict scattered across the ground like paper dolls. Cheering chants from above build louder. Conner soaks in the applause: It is the last time he will hear anything like it for a year. He knows the monotony will set in again, an unending series of work tasks broken only by his precious hours drawing inside the prison's hobby shop. But Conner will come back to the bulls again. He's married to this window to the outer world, this opportunity to make the faces on the other side see him as a captivating spectacle rather than a terrifying one.

"It's a challenge," he will tell the journalist later that afternoon, "and I'll be doing it as long as I can."

A NEW ASSEMBLY of bulls is steered to the chutes. The crowd's vigilance is drawn to eight prisoners strutting toward the stadium's center. Fighting for the title of All Around Cowboy, contenders know what this moment, called "Pinball," is about to bring: Each man steps into a plastic hula-hoop and waits for the unleashing of the bull. Most crouch on their ankles; two rest with palms on their knees, heads tucked down, knowing that victory will go to the last inmate standing.

A chute whips open. The first aggressor sent at the convicts is a blond middleweight with a high, gleaming back. He's quick but imprecise. He follows the rag-signals of his clown provokers; but he's hesitant. No taste for human devastation.

Round two.

The next bull's meaner. His coat is black bayou water and

his hooves are silver claws of hard, horny tissue. He barrels past the chute man, gathering a muscle-manic speed with his skull throwing forked hooks and wild haymakers. He plows half the convicts off their ground without touching them, blowing them back with the lean, raving force of his momentum.

An inmate on the east side of the action digs his boots in. He holds firm in his ring, determined to prove to the rodeo fans in West Feliciana Parish that he's tough as any jailbird comes. He won't look away from the prowling gomer: It trots, turns and charges. Its forehead fires down into the gnarled dust. Horns hit the jailbird hard under his heels, and the reemerging power train of grizzled tendons and grit launches the victim into an open sky. The jailbird lands far enough ahead to take a full run from the attacker across his ribs, the bestial mass no longer aware of him, loping fast at a neon scarf from the nearest bullfighter. Panicked breaths rush through the crowd. The downed inmate vaults back onto his feet. There is a delay before the applause booms. The jailbird rips his helmet off, takes three rage-ramped strides and winds his arm back, as if to hurl his gear through the hide and hair and all seven stomachs of the dominating stampeder. Laughing howls and hearty cheers are almost deafening now: The blaring exaltation of ancient arena life.

Yet the jailbird's antics hit the creature's sensory, instantly luring its hulked tonnage back. A clown senses the threat. He snaps his rodeo rag at the bull's head as it marauds by, a long, matted death dart thrusting at the jailbird. It's a charge. Nostrils close the distance. The helmet that had just been steadying on the jailbird's bicep falls limp along his thigh, brushing an odd beat against sprinting denim. The cheers taper off. The inmate is pushing so hard the spectators scarcely see his legs move. It's six full bull-lengths to the chutes. The predator's hooves have a graceful speed now, and against it the other's boots bang down desperately, again and again. Gasps pan north and south of the rafters. The jailbird takes one big leap, his hands catching the middle bar of a chute, shoulders jerking up, ribs and hips swaying, his good arm attacking the high line of iron, so that his entire body sweeps in a cradle rock—a fetal-slug lob up over the gate as the bull's horns pass inches from the back of the running man's knees.

The shouting Louisianans come unbuckled.

Event-goers have just recovered from the jailbird's gambit when ranchmen drop folding chairs and a card table in the middle of the arena. Four inmates strap on helmets and walk out. The game is "convict poker." Willing themselves for the table, the men sense a fresh galvanic pulse track through the audience. They hunker down in their seats to form a four-bodied cross of Kevlar and blue jeans. One grabs the deck to start dealing: A bullfighter clutching rags takes position behind his shoulder, another moving between his left eye and the patriotic chutes. The dealer perceives, through the cage of his helmet, wide billboards adorning each gate: Garvely Engine Co., Brown's Dairy, Coca-Cola, the Louisiana State Lottery. It's the lottery chute that opens all at once, blurred by a dirty, coal-peppered mass of rushing life aimed at the card table.

The last poker player's ass to touch chair-bottom is declared the winner.

The crowd readies for old school bull riding. The first seven inmates out of the gates go down in hurled turns, crashing the soil with their limbs wrapping a maimed deck of clods and parched bareness. The eighth convict to tighten down on the strap is Gary Lafleur. Chute men trigger the explosion and Lafleur is already flexing, his arms tearing himself back to the other's rank, flinty spine where beyond an unseen nexus of gravity whirls just out of reach. The legion of girth bucks up again, arching in a rugged spasm. The world comes back: Lafleur absorbs its jolt through his bone couplings. Hammering its hindquarters, the bull pitches north towards the chutes. Audience members muster a united voice. Lafleur is the first inmate to take three rocks. His opponent drives strong, heaving and half-tilting in the air—a moving sculpture of hesitant violence. The convict shifts, grips and clenches as rows of fans cry out. Four impacts and still riding. The animal cuts right and then straightens into a thick stump of surging duress: It's all kicks and intestinal huffing ahead of a red funnel of smoked flakes. The bull marshals another jump. Lafleur is cloaked in the stadium's fevered calls; but the brushy hide is slipping under him, tunneling out of the shape of his bent knee and cocked ankle, lashing on the pulled denim of his blue jeans. Lafleur's Kevlar vest, and the bones and vitals within it, drop hard on the arena floor. He lays prostrate for an instant before one of the bull's back legs lands down on his pelvis. The applause ebbs: Its roar tapers into broken hiccups.

The convict coils onto his side. He wills himself up before the clowns are even close; and the moans overhead roll in a symphony-saw crescendo back into cheers.

TWENTY-FIVE MINUTES BEFORE the national anthem was sung over the fences, a small group of reporters gathered around Warden Burl Cain, head of the Louisiana State Penitentiary and the true rodeo king of Angola. The facility Cain oversees spans eighteen thousand acres, surrounded on three of its sides by the Mississippi River and guarded at its north by Lake Killarney—full of nine and ten-foot alligators—and fortified by the Tunica Hills, ridgetops of ironwood, red cedar, holly and hickory: It's pure American jungle.

In 1950, *Time Magazine* called Angola "the bloodiest prison in America." Its walls held a cluster of human anger and despair. It was a place where the majority of inmates had nothing to live for and nothing to lose. Violence, rapes and suicides were endemic. By 1995, when Cain took over handling "the farm," the situation remained grim. The warden now admits he never wanted the job in the early days.

"This place was a slave plantation before the Civil War," Cain remarked offhandedly before the rodeo started. "Between that bondage and this prison, there's probably been more suffering on this piece of land than anywhere in the world."

Cain's main approach to stemming the misery has been to instill a philosophy of helping "lifers" find individual purposes within their damnation. Convicts with seven to ten years of good conduct begin to see doors open for them. Angola is a prison with an award-winning, inmate-written magazine for the public, an inmate-operated, FCC-licensed radio station heard throughout St. Francisville, seven inmate bands that perform at events, inmate dog breeders, inmate horse trainers, inmate hospice workers and inmate seminary specialists. In Cain's Angola, when a convict dies and family fails to claim the body, the man is laid out in a coffin crafted by inmates, put in a horse-drawn carriage for a jazz funeral march led by inmate musicians, eulogized by an ordained inmate deacon and then lowered into a cemetery plot under a clean, white headstone fashioned by fellow prisoners.

Today's sold-out prison rodeo is a colossal manifestation of the new atmosphere Cain has created. Chatting with reporters, the warden can gaze out at the ocean of inmate craft booths: Ornamented belts, polished rocking chairs, refined wood bowls, handmade jewelry and an array of paintings. Cain's bustling bazaar is the only place where Louisianans can freely talk with armed robbers, drug traffickers and murderers. Working the fields of Angola, inmates make pennies an hour; many spend that money on materials for their crafts and are allowed to keep eighty percent of each sale. It is not just the inmates facing the bulls and broncs who have been looking forward to this moment all year it's also the army of creative hopefuls spanning the craft market.

"Part of 'corrections' is correcting behavior," Cain told three newspaper journalists and two camera crews before the event. "You can't change prisoners by tormenting and torturing them: People work on reward systems. They earn their way into these events by good conduct. In fact, they have to have very good conduct."

A television reporter turned to a familiar question for Cain, a criticism that has been raised by several investigative journalists out of New York: He asked the warden if it was true that he and his staff intentionally push evangelical Christianity on a trapped audience within the prison's walls. The controversy, now a decade in the running, has made Cain a minor media star in the South.

With data indicating Cain's tenure at Angola has reduced violence and suicides, the warden has stood his ground with few apologies. This day was no different.

"We're not encouraging one religion over another," Cain responded. "But we do find that religion in general is important because it helps teach a moral component...People who are criminals are bullies and takers; they're out there raping and robbing...We feel if they have a moral component, they won't want to do those things to others."

Pointing out toward the craft fair, he added, "These men get really offended if someone shoplifts from them during the event, which happens, and we have to laugh at them because that's what they did to others. Now they know how it feels."

A young female reporter who traveled more than half way around the world from Angola, Africa, informed Cain he is a figure of admiration in her country. She asked him to look into her cameraman's lens and send a message to the nation about dealing with criminality. For an instant the old media veteran looked caught off guard. Focusing, Cain brought his face to meet the camera as he summarized his philosophy that compassion is the shepherd's rod that truly leads the lost.

With seconds to go before the start of the rodeo, the motley media group trailed off for the arena. One newspaper journalist stayed back for a moment, listening to the force in Cain's voice dissipate as he began to relax in the blinding daylight.

"Just wanted to ask one more question," the journalist said. "For the inmates who are actually going to climb on to the bulls and broncs in a few minutes, what would you say this means to them?"

Cain's snowy eyebrows lifted. "Well, it's almost immeasurable," he observed in a quieting rasp. "For one moment, they get to be a hero. They actually have people clapping and cheering for them. Listen, a lot of these men have never had anyone root for them in their entire life. It's not about a rodeo—it's about changing people."

"Are a good number of the inmates who are going to lay it all out there in the arena ever getting out?"

The warden turned his head with gentle contemplation rustling in his eyelids. "No," he answered mutedly. "No, we buried fifty-two last year and we released twenty-eight, and that's pretty much how it goes."

INSIDE THE ARENA, the crowd is craving Guts and Glory, the final event that pits thirteen free-ranging convicts against the defensive arsenal of one of Lewis and Dunn's biggest bulls. The challenger trots out. Its Minotaur head looks Grecian, the bone-white face hinged to a massive goiter-hump darker than a southern night. Long-legged, raven black, it bolts past the gate with crimson-painted horns flashing like wet blood in the sunlight. The inmates shift together. They move as a probing pack of striped wranglers as the wind sweeps under paper fins stapled to their backs. The dare is to grab a scarlet chit between the bull's horns. Marlon "The Tank" Brown, looking happy and harmless in his floppy straw fishing hat, struts out ahead of the other offenders. He squares up with his Herculean prey in the east corner of the stadium. Brown has cheated the Devil fourteen times in this event. Now, the beast stops in front of him. They make eye contact. Brown plants his right foot back and drops the other knee forward, centering his gravity through the core of his wide hips. The bull stands perfectly still. The inmate's power is in his forward leg, his palms lightly tapping his concrete quads. The bull watches him. It digs a single hoof into the soil. Brown leans in, sparring, shadow dancing, slightly feigning a phantom charge. Dirt explodes. There's a dash from the ebony hull of tendons and tail, plowing in a half-hook motion along the fence that turns and smashes horns into Brown's right side: Marlon "The Tank" is hammered onto his stomach and elbows.

The animal head-swats Brown again before making a gallop at the pack of inmates. Brown rolls by an awning shadow and pair of truck tracks flattened on the scud. He lurches to his feet, bounding from the arena's corner out under the cloudless blue sky. Cheers are trumpeting: Brown hears them, sporadic, loud, random, pulsing. The bull moves north. Convicts are bobbing and weaving as Brown canters through them. Just under the announcers, he again meets that pale skull on black, lifted muscles. Its eyes look centuries old. The scarlet chit remains on its forehead, a beckoning blood-bump that's yet to be grazed. Cowhands and convicts in white Stetsons drape the nearest chute. Brown opens himself up. The bull's crushing collarbone drives, its sidelong horns run savaging at the convict's center, his own knees buckling and his ankles sliding— and the bright, scarlet chit firing in.

JOHN EASLEY WATCHES the collision from his seat. He is inundated by a Louisiana-loud applause for the revelation of Brown's battered arm lifting the chit up, triumphant, for the fifteenth time. Easley smiles. A longtime college instructor, the man is tall, solid, steely haired and a bad fit for retirement. His passion for teaching real-world job skills makes him an ideal fit to run vocational teaching at Angola Prison. One of Easley's main projects is overseeing Angola's Offender Teaching Offender Inmate Mentor Program. Easley and Warden Cain agree this new endeavor is breaking ground for the future of

American corrections. They know the public might be surprised to learn that at Angola Prison, once called "the Alcatraz of the South," even inmates sentenced to life can earn enough good conduct credits, and take enough satellite college courses, to become certified adjunct college instructors through the Louisiana Community and Technical College System. While these master mechanics and electricians will never teach general students in a classroom, they do impart their knowledge to a group of men they have a better chance of reaching than anyone else—young, nonviolent inmates serving short prison terms through the Orleans Parish court system. The program creates a world where instructors are convicts in need of a mission and students are drug addicts and former gang members in need of certified job skills and unflinching guidance. It is a plan in full motion to keep the students from ending up permanent residents within the Louisiana criminal justice landscape.

For all of the talk about the "tough-on-crime South," Cain, Easley and the staff at the Louisiana State Penitentiary have been testing new ways to pull meaning from tragedy and move away from failed rehabilitation methods. The program is funded entirely by ticket sales from the Angola Prison Rodeo, offering it a shield from state budget woes and those who criticize spending tax dollars on criminals.

One of the men Easley relies on to make inmate mentoring a success is John Sheehan, a model prisoner for twenty-seven years who's earned two master's degrees inside of Angola. Sheehan has no difficulty explaining why the re-entry program is just as important to its instructors as the students it's attempting to save.

"This is a chance for us to give back," Sheehan says. "I've

been in this place a long time, and if I can do something to help a young man who's just come into the system not end up the same way, that's what I want to do. Plus, we all have family members on the outside, and we don't want them to become victims of crimes, either. This is our chance to play a role in breaking the cycle."

Angola's inmate mentoring started in May of 2010. Today's prison rodeo lands just shy of the program's third anniversary. So far, twenty-three men have graduated its curriculum and gone back to life beyond the walls. Only three have re-offended. Seven of the graduates have been to Baton Rouge to take the national Automotive Service Excellence certification test, which would allow them to work as professional mechanics.

All seven former inmates passed.

Angola's staff attributes the program's success largely to its inmate mentors, who are looking beyond their own life sentences to try to stop new ones from getting handed to the students. The prison's assistant warden, Gary Young, has been so impressed by these mentors that it causes hesitant pauses when he writes news bulletins for the institution.

"When it comes to some of them, I don't even like to use the term 'offender,'" Young admits. "John Sheehan is not an 'offender.' He hasn't done anything to offend me. It's the language we use in corrections, but it doesn't always tell the story."

The same thought will echo in Young's mind when, a month later, a lethal tornado destroys several towns outside Oklahoma City and inmates from Angola's re-entry programs choose to donate nearly $4,000 of their own money to its victims. The gesture was antithetical to self-involved "criminal thinking;"

but, to a man, change almost never equals second chances in Louisiana's current political climate. For John Easley, this point is punctuated whenever he thinks of Shelby Arabie, an inmate he knows to be a leader in prison's job training and mentoring efforts.

In 1984, Arabie was involved in a drug deal that went spiraling out of control. He was robbed, pistol-whipped and tied-up by men posing as buyers from Mississippi. When Arabie managed to get loose and chase his attackers, a second confrontation resulted in him firing a single pistol shot: The lone discharge took the life of one of his ambushers. Despite serious misgivings from Arabie's trial judge, prosecutors used the jury system and appellate court to get the small-time marijuana dealer sentenced to life without parole. Over the course of twenty-nine years behind bars, Arabie has turned into one of the most respected and trusted men walking the grounds of Angola. He earned his GED and became a certified computer technician. From attitude to work ethic, he's proved an exemplary prisoner on every level. Arabie was a crucial partner in developing Angola's inmate-mentoring program. When Hurricane Katrina brought terror and social breakdown to Louisiana in 2005, Angola Prison's staff had the confidence to take Arabie and six other inmates with them on the relief efforts. Cain later told *The Times-Picayune* newspaper that Arabie played a crucial role in their mission: "He kept our generators running for other prisons," the warden said to reporter Jan Moller. "He could do what we couldn't do—our own staff; and he willingly helped and taught others."

The only hope for a man sentenced to life without parole in Louisiana is an official pardon from the governor. Angola's staff views Arabie as a prime example of state corrections helping an inmate correct himself; and so a hearing was granted for Arabie before the Louisiana Board of Pardons in August of 2011. Arabie carried with him a strong letter of support from Cain, one of only three recommendations for pardon the warden has issued in his career. An unexpected face also showed up to urge Arabie's release: Ashley Posey, the daughter of the man he had killed. Posey told the pardon board she is convinced Arabie is not the same man who engaged in an armed duel with her father in 1984. She believes he deserves a second chance at life. The board of pardons cast a five-to-zero vote to recommend Arabie for clemency and declare him ready for parole.

Two years later, as citizens mull around the inmate craft fair, Louisiana Governor Bobby Jindal still has not acted on the board's recommendation to pardon Arabie. An investigation by *The Times-Picayune* suggested that out of four hundred and fifteen recommendations the board made to pardon inmates in prison, Jindal released just one person. He denied thirty-six more recommendations, and has simply failed to take any action at all on the other three hundred and seventy-eight, including Arabie.

Louisiana currently has one of the highest incarceration rates per capita in the United States.

"It can be really difficult to work so closely with some of the men you know are truly rehabilitated, and could be good, productive citizens, but will never get out because of our mandatory sentencing laws," Easley acknowledges. "Some of these guys came from backgrounds you wouldn't believe. They never heard one positive thing from anyone before they came here. That's not to make excuses for what they did, because in the end individuals know the difference between right and wrong. But we've got men who have been in here for decades and proved they're not only skilled laborers, but also that they have changed. It is hard to see the outstanding ones not get a chance. A lot of people who've never been around these inmates could never imagine feeling sorry for them; but when you get to know them on a one-on-one basis—the ones who are truly rehabilitated—you'd be surprised how it changes the way you feel."

CHAPTER 7

June, Roseville, California: Causalities

YOU WOULDN'T LOOK twice at him.

In the world of fishing, there is nothing lower than his kind—a vulture-minded angler who seeks out other sportsmen's best biting spots and then crowds them off the plate. Around the lakes, rivers and streams of Placer County, California, there are few things a fisherman hates more than an envious skulker who's too unmotivated to find his own trout or catfish, instead stalking your honey spot with a beer in hand, swooping in from a distance with his cheating-ass live minnows to trump your tail spinners. And that is exactly what the 37-year-old stranger looks like on this June afternoon, a shameless spot-spy, a lazy bastard, a ne'er-do-well of the rod and reel, with his handlebar mustache over chin scruff, his worn-out ball cap holding down a Bostonian hair-lick from the 1970s, his old flannel clad on a stretched, dirty blue T-shirt, and his crinkled, second-rate cigarettes popping out of a khaki shorts pocket—conspicuous lung darts readied for the draw. Sixty miles south in the California Delta, there's not an angler on the docks who would turn their back on him, because any seasoned bass pro knows a worthless potlicker when he sees one.

But it's just his cover.

This man who looks like a cross between a mangy Walmart warrior and lowdown fisherman is actually Roseville narcotics detective Bret Brzyscz, who needs only a pressed uniform, a clean shave and haircut to mirror his appearance when he was named Roseville's Police Officer of the Year. Lately, Brzyscz's partners, Sgt. Dave Buelow and detectives Andy Palmore and Chad Baumann, have been resembling members of an outlaw motorcycle gang. But Brzyscz has opted for a different look: The appearance of an offbeat, chain-smoking, summer-bum lake lackey. When it comes to undercover work, you don't necessarily have to look like a thug in Brzyscz's estimation, you just have to look like "not a cop."

The detective has had ten years to think about a cover that won't draw attention. Brzyscz's stakeout look may be original but it is his memory that he's known for. His nickname around the department is "Bret Query," due to the suspicion his brain's an organic search engine capable of connecting any name to its respective mug shot within Roseville's contained landscape of Norteños, Sureños, Peckerwoods, solo dealers and serial burglars.

Brzyscz glances across Hickory Street at the address he's been monitoring for a week. As if following a stage direction, his suspect, Forrest Locke, wanders out of an open garage into the detective's field of vision. The June heat feels like it's trying to make windows soften. Hoisting a cell phone to his ear, Locke flexes his bare-chested muscles, sunlight tracing the weaves of his tattoos. Locke is a 24-year-old who already has convictions for theft, auto theft and fighting with police officers. In April 2010, Locke was arrested for possession of narcotics and carrying burglars' tools. That case was ultimately pled down, though Locke earned sixteen months in state prison. By March 2011 he was back on the streets and under arrest again, this time for brawling with a Roseville cop. A week ago, Locke came off Post Release Community Supervision for his struggle with that officer. Prior to California passing Realignment, Locke could have faced prison time for fighting with a police officer. However, the language of AB 109 now classifies California Penal Code 69, fighting with peace officers, as a "nonviolent" offense under the law. In the coming months, Locke will be arrested on charges of beating a man on Conroy Lane until he is hospitalized and then, just three nights later, beating and robbing a different man in the same part of the city.

And it is that propensity for violence that has Roseville cops worried about Locke. At this moment they are not the only ones. The main reason that the department's Vice and Narcotics Enforcement Team has been watching him involves allegations that he's recently been intimidating his neighbors.

"We've gotten reports he's been menacing residents in the area who notice the drug traffic coming and going," Brzyscz mentioned while looking over intelligence in the morning. "I guess when he was on parole, he kept to himself and left people alone; but since he's been off he's been trying to scare people on the block. Really tough guy—a 24-year-old throwing threatening stares at men and women in their sixties."

Now, Brzyscz's eyes follow the small, shifting circles that Locke's sneakers beat into the lawn. The young man keeps a cell phone to his ear. He speaks rapidly, glancing up and down the street. A woman in her late forties cranes back on an old sofa jutting from the garage onto the driveway slab. She absorbs the warmth, hanging out at the stash house because her daughter, Cassandra Flor, is Locke's girlfriend.

"I've got eyes on the target," Brzyscz says into his radio. "He's on the phone. He's looking all around. There's also an adult female in the garage and there's a young juvenile running around, probably around four years old."

Locke clicks his phone off and moves out of view. Brzyscz sits tight. Detectives Buelow, Palmore and Baumann are in surveillance positions north of Hickory Street. Moments later Locke emerges from the garage dressed in shorts and a long, red shirt. His cell phone is back at the side of his head. He paces down the sidewalk, glancing long over his shoulder.

Brzyscz presses down on his radio: "Target is on the move, northbound on Hickory Street toward Switchman Drive. He's talking to someone on the phone. His head is really swiveling. He's looking around everywhere."

Locke struts by Brzyscz, moving past Washbash Way and then crossing Chisum Court.

"I see him," Baumann says from his position near Elm Street. The detective watches Locke cut through a cluster of brush along a retaining wall, moving into a drug store parking lot.

"He's coming up to the front of the Walgreens at Main Street and Foothills," Baumann puts on the radio, firing his ignition and pulling down Switchman Drive. Sunlight whitens the contours of his dashboard. Baumann wheels right. He watches Locke stroll to the Walgreens entrance. Rolling out of a U-turn into a gas station, the detective sees Locke approach a waiting car. Behind the wheel is 19-year-old Derek Snider. It happens in an instant: Locke reaches into the passenger window and then Snider's car is pulling out of the parking lot again.

"We've got a sale," Baumann informs his partners. "Bret, target's heading back to you."

Buelow, the team leader, asks two agents in an unmarked truck to follow as Snider drives onto Roseville's main street. Ahead is "Old Town," the original city, the saloon-studded railroad core, the Prohibition-era rat trap of two-story blocks whose masonry runs in earthen hues until their bricks halt near the train yard's swollen lip of gravel. Pale stucco on the Barker Hotel boils in the sun. Salmon-leafed alder branches burgeon along Pacific Street under the district's water tower, ahead of hairy weeds shouldering fallow through chain link— as if craning in a long, brittle reach for the steel rails that push north. Roseville leaders have a vision for this landscape: They see a historic quarter where shades of the past merge with fashions of the future, creating a trendy entertainment scene where commerce can thrive. But Old Town's little storefronts occupied by novel businesses are one reality. The Roseville Hotel and the Barker Hotel, with their broken door locks, clogged gagging sinks, cracked walls and sludge-sketched starfishes under roach legs, is a lesser known but equally felt truth. The Barker Hotel often has two working toilets for forty-five apartments. The Roseville Hotel has tenants ripping floors up and conversing with the Devil. The "flop houses" are aged, white clods riddled in window trash and torn screens that peak behind phallic sycamores. Just east of them is the chewed, red stone of the city's oldest building, the 1878 Odd Fellows Hall, now a tenant den where addicts are accused of breaking apart smoke detectors so methamphetamine mist can plume freely in their rooms.

Old Town is almost in Snider's windshield when officers

Mike Ryland and Mike Sidebottom stop him for a missing plate. Snider coasts into the parking lot of a 7-Eleven on Main Street where splintered-faced vagrants line up to use the city's last working pay phone. Ryland is Brzyscz's former partner on night patrols, and there's not a narco niche in the car that will get by him and Sidebottom. Finding Locke's product in the vehicle will put the final touches on a search warrant Brzyscz is writing for the house on Hickory Street.

The midday sun is blinding over Locke's neighborhood. Brzyscz waits. Locke comes marching down Switchman Street flanked by two young men. Ryland's voice breaks over the main dispatch channel, calling an arrest code for Derek Snider. Brzyscz glances down, nodding to himself. A second later his cell phone rings.

"What do you got?"

"Heroin," Ryland says.

Brzyscz watches Locke go sauntering back into his house. Moments later he reemerges with Cassandra Flor and her mother. The three of them load into a silver minivan.

"Target's on the move in a van," Brzyscz calls through his receiver. "Heading down Hickory." The detective listens to his partners engage in a covert choreography of shifting cars, until Locke is ultimately pulled over in full view of the Roseville Police Department. Brzyscz knows the larger stash of heroin is inside the house. He wonders if Locke had enough time to send a text message to the young men inside before the other detectives pulled him out of the van. If the product gets flushed down a toilet, nothing can be done.

Brzyscz's phone rings again.

"Forrest is going to jail," Buelow's voice says on the other end of the line. "We're on our way to lock down the house. As soon as we get there, finish the warrant."

Moments later, Locke's neighborhood sees the men coming—sunglasses, thick beards, dark tactical vests strapped over T-shirts. The word "police" runs in wasp-yellow lettering across their backs. Buelow is ahead. As they move up Locke's driveway, a patrol cruiser rolls up with Cassandra Flor in its back seat.

Brzyscz starts his truck up. Within thirty minutes his warrant is signed by a Placer County judge. Before the detective even reaches the first floor of the courthouse he calls Buelow. "Yeah, we've got it," he says. "Start searching."

As the team gets to work, Brzyscz drives to the police station to meet Locke face to face. He strolls through the open hallway to the interview room. The door opens. When he walks in, Locke slowly looks up at the detective who made the case against him, the man who developed the leads, who worked with the confidential witnesses, who sat on his house for days and then wrote a concrete warrant—an investigator dressed like a dock-dwelling, cigarette-bumming, just-out-of-bed, totally worthless fisherman.

Back at Locke's house, Buelow finds the heroin stash on the top shelf in an old shed in the backyard. Cassandra Flor is arrested in connection to possession of heroin for sale. When a newspaper photographer snaps a shot of Flor led out in handcuffs, he knows his readers will be surprised by the image: She is young, blond and pretty. Her clothes are clean, tidy-looking. The photographer knows the girl will strike Roseville residents as a face they'd expect to see working at Pottery Barn or Beach Hut Deli, rather than being led around in cuffs in connection to heroin. But the horse stash is here, in the same house where Flor is living with her 4-year-old daughter and infant child; and Forrest Locke, who has just graduated PRSC weeks before, is now officially charged with dealing black tar around the city.

The operation was textbook from start to finish; and it's exactly the type of enforcement detail that's increasingly under fire from groups who consider themselves justice reformists. Buelow knows that any cop working narcotics in California is now in the sightline of a national magnifying glass because of the state's experiment with Realignment. Buelow is also aware that tomorrow morning, just twenty-eight miles south in downtown Sacramento, the newest independent data on Realignment will be unveiled at a forum by the Public Policy Institute of California. Buelow won't be there. He and his detectives have reports to write, follow-up investigations to conduct—a catered, air-conditioned conference room is not in the cards for them. And so the sergeant won't be in the audience during the panel discussion, when Stanislaus County Sheriff Adam Christianson opens up about the staggering amount of crime sweeping through his community because of methamphetamine. Buelow won't hear Christianson wearily exclaim that meth is triggering double-digit increases in property crimes for the families, businesses and farmers he is charged with protecting, nor will he hear the sheriff recount that, the week before, an entire system of traffic lights and signals at the Crows Landing Air Station was stolen by meth addicts.

"They took all of that," Christianson will emphasize. "Just, all gone—because it's metal."

Buelow also won't hear Christianson observe that "dealing

with Realignment is like drinking from a fire hose." And while Buelow will see none of it, he does wonder about public views around offenders like Forrest Locke—drug users circulating through PRCS programs with known propensities for violence.

"Forrest Locke is a failure of Realignment," Buelow remarks. "But he won't go down on paper that way because of how the system is set up."

Buelow can say that and it cannot be disputed; but in the eyes of a national organization such as Law Enforcement Against Prohibition, or LEAP, the failures around addicts like Forrest Locke lie more with state and federal anti-drug laws and decisions to fund narcotics enforcement teams. Comprised of about one-hundred and twenty retired American police officers, correctional officers, prosecutors and judges—and a handful of working cops and international law enforcement personnel— LEAP advocates legalizing and regulating all narcotics. The group believes its social shift would reduce violence around illegal trafficking and gang warfare while diverting more resources into rehabilitation programs. LEAP is also convinced its sea change will lower the number of fatal overdoses and remove the criminal justice stressors that hinder longtime addicts from rebuilding their lives. Addiction is not an entity that can be defeated in a "war." Wars are won through force of arms. Addiction is a malignancy of the human spirit. For those who are wading their way out of it, finding a good job with felonies on your record, paying your bills with judicial fines over your head and trying to manage an employment schedule while being forced to attend court-mandated classes can add to the mire of stress an addict pushes back against while trying to avoid relapse.

Many California narcotics detectives know LEAP's argument appeals to a segment of the public that understands addiction through the storytelling of films such as "Less Than Zero," "The Basketball Dairies" and "Permanent Midnight." But while most Hollywood portrayals of addiction focus on a user's life disintegrating, newly released statistics show the impacts—especially around Buelow's jurisdiction—go beyond individual bloodstreams and are hardwired to a wider spectrum of tragedy and victimization. Last week, the President's Office of National Drug Control Policy released a study linking drug use to overall crime patterns in the city of Sacramento, ten minutes down the freeway from Roseville. The report determined that in 2011 more than eighty-two percent of suspects arrested in Sacramento for all manner of crimes tested positive for drug use.

Roseville has its own figure to illuminate the nexus between drug addiction and crime, one that's tied directly to Realignment arrestees like Forrest Locke. According to data transferred from California's department of corrections to the Placer County Probation Department, ninety-two percent of the area's new Post Release Community Supervision offenders were addicted to drugs or alcohol at the time they were apprehended: Those cases often involved far more than the drugs themselves, delving into convictions for property crime, identity theft, child endangerment and domestic violence.

While methamphetamine, heroin and crack are fueling a great deal of crimes against citizens in cities like Sacramento and Roseville, members of LEAP are not convinced that police narcotics squads are stemming the tide by going after traffickers. James Gray was the federal prosecutor who, in 1978, indicted the largest heroin smuggling case in Central California's history.

He went on to spend twenty-five years as a superior court judge in Orange County, California. Gray's time on the bench caused him to disavow the mission parameters he had once embraced as a federal prosecutor.

"What I saw in my court is that no matter how many times we arrested, convicted and sentenced big-time drug dealers, it never ended the supply," Gray remembers. "No, every time it just opened a job opportunity for someone else. The other thing I noticed was the tougher we got on drug crime, the worse we did on prosecuting other things like violent crimes and rapes. United States prosecutors were twice as successful at prosecuting homicides in 1980 than we are now, the year before Ronald Regan ramped up 'the war on drugs.'"

In Gray's opinion, changing tactics against drug-inspired crime could be critical to solving the nation's problem with prison overcrowding.

"The key is for law enforcement to separate what people actually do from what they put in their bodies," Gray says. "When drug users engage in behavior that puts the public at risk, like driving under the influence, property crimes and acts of violence, those instances will be prosecuted as criminal events. Admittedly, the police would be dealing with a lot of the same people they were dealing with before, but this tactic would weed out the people who are using drugs but not causing harm to others."

LEAP envisions a law enforcement landscape across the U.S. where narcotics teams are re-assigned to protective patrol or investigative details for crimes drug addicts commit. LEAP is confident retooling police strategies would result in fewer unnecessary incarcerations and high overall conviction rates for transgressions pursued.

However, there is no shortage of law enforcement officers who view LEAP's would-be methods as non-preventative and entirely reactive: If police officers and sheriff's deputies working in the greater Sacramento region know that eighty-two percent of all crimes are committed by addicts, then it's likely that arresting those individuals on drug charges—be it to get them forced treatment or simply removed from the streets for a time—is proactively stopping a certain number of citizens from being victims.

At this very moment, Buelow's team is investigating a crew of Roseville heroin dealers who have threatened to kill a witness in a trafficking case. When the young men are arrested in a few weeks, they'll be in possession of semi-automatic pistols, a shotgun and cell phones that showcase them smiling and holding up AK-47s. Court testimony from Detective Palmore will ultimately link them to selling laced heroin that killed at least one young man. The group's arrest will happen the same week that three assailants wearing clown masks put a gun to a pedestrian's head near Old Town Roseville, and then pistol-whip him in the face before ripping away his ball cap, his sneakers and his smart phone. Police also suspect a drug crew in that encounter.

If the narcotics-sanctioned world that members of LEAP advocate comes about but fails to eliminate a sliver of the black market, then detectives like Buelow and Brzyscz fear they will continue to deal with violent aftershocks while having few legal avenues left for arresting suspects engaged in the carnage.

"There's the issue of trying to address the problems from some of these individuals before they commit certain crimes,"

Buelow observes. "If our team hits a ring of heroin-addicted dealers that is rolling around our city with guns, and we're able to get them into custody, then we've probably prevented an armed robbery or an act of violence before it's happened."

And the final part of the equation for Buelow and his team is a nexus that cuts straight through the center of innocence when it comes to the link between drug addiction and child abuse. All of the Roseville investigators have seen it. In just a few months, Detective Palmore will be executing a warrant at a drug house and be hit by the reality again. He'll walk in, stop and brace his senses against the overpowering odor of feces, urine, soiled clothes, fouled bodies and cannabis. There will be no working heat for the three small children living within the house's bantam dimensions alongside a group of adults selling large quantities of reefer, and as Palmore keeps walking he'll see the menagerie of exposed electrical wire, leaking pipes, protruding nails, barbed broken counter tiles, scurrying roaches in drawers, spades of spiders, gang graffiti on walls and random underfed dogs; and when he comes into the kids' bedroom he will be ready to call Child Protective Services, after finding that all three little ones are forced to sleep on an indented mattress covered in grime and fresh urine stains—with one child escaping the smell by sleeping on a pile of filthy clothes peppered in cockroach corpses. The living conditions Palmore will document in his child endangerment case do not even consider, on paper, the threat of the house falling victim to an armed marijuana robbery from gang members in the area.

"Children are always abandoned in the drug culture," Buelow says. "Children are the number one thing that should make people ask themselves if this is a victimless crime.

Hardcore addicts can't be adequate parents. Child abuse and child endangerment cases happen all the time when we go into these houses, and the addicts keep the kids trapped in situations that are extremely hazardous to their health and development. They are also making sure the next generation gets brought up learning to take from society and to have a totally different moral compass than the rest of us."

The viewfinder into children and tragedy is one that both LEAP members such as Judge Gray and narcotics agents like Dave Buelow are constantly staring into. Each man agrees America's drug culture is chewing up the lives of the young and defenseless. Gray is convinced legalization would halt the phenomenon of street dealers and gangs recruiting teens and even pre-teens into doorways of self-evaporation.

"The war on drugs is a failure, but we're still fighting it primarily because of children," Gray acknowledges. "No one wants to see kids pulled into this totally destructive lifestyle. But you have to ask yourself this: When a dealer manages to recruit a 16-year-old to sell for him, who in that community do you think that 16-year-old will turn around and start selling to? The answer is much younger children. That cycle playing out, over and over, is an image that should bring tears to your eyes."

While Buelow's team believes the priority should be stopping the predatory dealers in those scenarios, they agree there's plenty of numbing realities around the drug world. In the coming weeks, the detectives will stand over the bodies of six different young people from Roseville, lost forever to heroin or opiate overdoses, and the reasons will fade into a passing blur of spoons on dirty carpets and toilets filled with needles.

THE NEXT MORNING Katie Tempesta and Lynne Brown walk into the historic Ransohoff building in downtown Sacramento. Katie has traveled half the day to attend a forum by the Public Policy Institute of California showcasing its latest data on Realignment. The PPIC is a nonprofit, nonpolitical research group tracking the impacts of AB 109 since it was passed. The key speaker will be Dr. Magnus Lofstrom, an economist who's become the foremost expert on statistics around the new law. Katie knows Lofstrom's panel includes one woman she's been getting to know, ungratefully, and another woman she very much wants to speak with.

Lofstrom takes the podium. He moves his contemplative look across the crowd. The same federal judges who ruled that California's prisons are unconstitutional have just issued a new order for the state to release nearly ten thousand prison inmates from custody by the end of the year. Realignment had been California Governor Jerry Brown's main strategy to avoid such a mass release of felons; but Lofstrom's data suggests that, since the law went into effect, the increase in California's county jail populations has not been matched by the decline of inmates in its state prisons. Tired of waiting for the results they had mandated, the federal judges are threatening what most California policy makers considered "the nuclear option." Lofstrom and the PPIC did not foresee such a ruling being issued on the eve of their Realignment symposium. The professor begins highlighting his newest research around AB 109, telling the audience that while Realignment hasn't decreased prison populations enough to satisfy federal judges, it has sparked new overcrowding issues in county jails all over California.

"The latest data is that (Realignment) has raised the populations in county jails, overall, by nine percent," Lofstrom explains in his crisp Swedish accent. "Eighteen counties now face population caps, and sixteen counties are now operating above their maximum jail capacity, which is an increase of eleven counties from this time last year."

He adds that jail overcrowding has forced counties across California to put thirty-four thousand convicted criminals on Post Release Community Supervision, while many county jails have gotten so crowded they have had to allow prisoners to walk free by issuing ordered releases.

"Thirty-five counties have reported releasing inmates early now, in the latest data," Lofstrom observes.

Katie Tempesta and Lynne Brown look on during Lofstrom's presentation. When the professor turns the stage over to his panel, Katie's attention silently peaks. In addition to Stanislaus County Sheriff Adam Christianson, the discussion will also be steered by Fresno County Probation Chief Linda Penner and California State Senator Loni Hancock. It was Penner's department that was charged with monitoring Michael Cockrell, the man who murdered Katie's mother. The first question posed to the authorities is the obvious one: Is Realignment working?

"What I can tell you is that it has not been catastrophic and the sky has not fallen," Penner says to the crowd. "There have been incidents where bad things happened; but bad things were happening before, and at the end of the day we weren't going to cure that or exacerbate that in many ways with Realignment, so I think we need to face the music on that...When I look back at Realignment, I think probation is absolutely up for the job. I think we know how to hold people accountable and at the same time, know how to gear people to life changes...Sometimes— and you've all heard this— crisis can be the mother of invention, and I think that's where we're at: We had a crisis, we had to react to that crisis, and I think we did that as gracefully as we could, and as thoughtfully as we could."

Katie takes tense breaths as she listens to the head of the very agency in charge of watching her mother's killer use the word "mother" to apparently downplay a few "bad things." Katie sits rigidly. Every muscle she has straightens hard. Her mouth is cinched. She's smoldering. "Lies," she whispers from the back of her lungs. "All I hear are lies." She fights to control her heartbeats. She concentrates on the panel. The next person to talk is Loni Hancock, chair of the Senate's public safety committee, a woman who has voted to kill every bill that Advocates for Public Safety has written to amend AB 109.

"I think that for a paradigm shift in the way we think about, organize and fund a major public system, it is going extraordinary well," Hancock says. "Sure, there are a few counties that really want to turn back the clock. Their representatives come to my committee with a bill," she pauses, slightly chuckling, "every couple of weeks, to send more prisoners back to the state: Never, by the way, followed by any of the money that the state put in the Constitution for them, but to erode Realignment; and we've been watching that, and I'm happy to say that that hasn't happened. But many more (counties) are stepping up to the plate and really looking at how they manage their jails, and how they think about their corrections problems, and are doing a remarkable job, and then there are some counties that did quite well originally, and they are thriving...In a former life I was a social psychologist, and we used to say, 'Change is painful. People never change, unless continuing the way they are is more painful than the pain of change;' and we were there in California."

The next question directed to the panel involves rising crime rates. Katie is in her chair, locked in a rigid watchfulness.

"Well, if you look at the data I've seen, crime is still at a forty-percent low in California," Hancock points out. "It's had a little uptick recently…this is why we need data everybody; because otherwise we're deconstructing anecdotal evidence all the time, and it leads to opportunities to erode the basis for Realignment. Now, I'm only going to say that I responded to a news story," she brings her hand up, conjuring in the air, "'Horrors, horrors, Realignment, murder,'" she mocks, "And I found the article didn't say it (was about a county with a federal court cap on its jail population), and had been court-capped for twenty-one years. And it turns out this individual had had their probation or parole revoked something like eleven times in the last year, and was released without a risk assessment." Hancock's words slow. "Then," her voice reclines in a resigned tone, "yes, there were consequences—so, jail management has a lot to do with it."

Katie works to control her breathing and calm her center as the moderator announces it is time for questions from the audience. Katie is the first person to raise her hand.

"Chief Penner, my question is for you," she says, standing up next to a PPIC assistant with a microphone. She focuses her internal charge into a quiet steadiness. "It was one of your PRCS offenders who brutally murdered my mom and tried to murder a Fresno police officer. I just would like to know, what's the criteria that is used to classify these 'low-level' offenders under Realignment?"

A spell of silent seconds elapses before Penner replies, "It's heart-wrenching—my heart goes out to you." The probation chief quickly delves into complexities around California probation and parole, landing on the conclusion, "some cases are going to result in tragic victimization." She reminds Katie that the criteria around who qualifies for PRCS and new forms of supervised release were engineered by the state. Penner also acknowledges aloud—for the only instant in the entire forum— that while Realignment calls for "nonviolent, nonsexual and non-serious offenders" to be monitored by the counties, there is a reality that some of these convicts have violent acts, serious crimes and sexual assaults in their past. "It's the instant offense that guides the individual to Post Release Community Supervision," Penner observes. With a note of sympathy in her voice, she looks at Katie and adds, "Maybe you could come find your way to me after the event."

Katie plans to do just that: Within minutes of the forum adjourning she walks directly over to Penner who is at back table near the exit.

"Which case are you talking about?" Penner inquires, looking up from her purse.

With a cautious, nearly professional demeanor Katie answers, "The killer is Michael Cockrell. He had—"

"Yes, I'm very familiar with that case," Penner interjects, "and I'm sorry about the tragedy your family has gone through."

"I just had a question about the exclusion list," Katie continues. "He was sentenced for a crime on the exclusion list after AB 109 passed."

"What was the offense?" Penner asks.

Katie takes an imperceptible breath before saying, "He

was convicted of viciously beating his pregnant girlfriend; but because of the exclusionary lists, he was put on PRCS."

"Listen, I never agreed with domestic violence being on the exclusion list, myself," Penner stresses. "I know that when someone is given a state prison term for domestic violence, in California, they could only have done the worst kind of violence, and done it repeatedly. Those are the only domestic violence defendants that really get sent to prison here." Pausing, the chief lifts her shoulders at a loss. "I mean, that's just the way it is," she says. "So, for them to put domestic violence on the list I thought was a mistake. It seems like that was done simply for the purpose of getting the prison population down more, but I was never for them putting that crime on the list."

Penner hands Katie a business card, asking, "Would you like to come talk to me more next week in Fresno?"

Katie takes the card without uttering a word.

Penner excuses herself. Katie turns and sees Lynne Brown walking toward her, and as her mentor approaches the larynx constricts, the tears blink out.

"Come on, let's get you some fresh air," Lynne whispers, putting her arm around Katie. "You did a great job. If it hadn't been for your question, the whole issue of the 'non, non, nons' never even would have come up today at all. Come on, you did really well."

Katie moves outside under the old Ransohoff's canopy. The Sacramento Cathedral is now in front of her, a shinbone pillar of salt fragmented in daylight, blotting out almost everything in her vision. The heat thickens. Flaring sun-beads skip along a trifecta of gold crosses in the sky. Saint Joseph and Saint Anthony guard the church's door, their delicate marble hands signaling to a bower of trees that tunnels to the north face of the Capitol: Katie can see the glaring blocked granite under its doors; but she remains in front of the cathedral, near a relief of Our Lady of Mount Carmel. The vision is pearled satin in the sun, with a gently chiseled face closing restful eyes as she holds an infant up to her cheeks. Mother and child.

Katie feels attorneys and political aides brush by her, fumbling with their briefcases, lifting their cell phones.

"They are going to keep looking me in the eye," Katie says with her energy returning. "When they want to say all of their misrepresentations, and all of their speeches where they don't even utter the word 'victim' once, they are going to have to do it while they look directly at me; because I'm not going away."

CHAPTER 8

Fall leaves and gunfire

HE SITS on the park bench, rocking back and forth. A wince tightens sun-chapped skin on the tiny spurs of his cheekbones. The line of his back is perfectly still. Inner whispers and circulating chemicals show in every crevice of his waiting expression—in the raw, grimy follicles along his eyelids, in the tangled palm of oily blond hair. His lips sputter. Words tremble through his mouth. From a blistered chin to flesh-clenched temples, his still look of diluted hunger ignores the strangers passing by. Blue eyes stay locked on nothing. Pedestrians glance from a distance, reluctantly scanning this man in his early forties slouched in a ballooned T-shirt and blotched jeans cinched to the narrow knobs of his starved-in hips. His pupils seem to empty straight into his blurred string of sentences, while he keeps nodding to himself, rocking faster and faster. His words cut through the warm morning air.

Behind the cheaply painted bench, over a hedge and a sidelong magnolia, a row of withered palm trees press against the west corner of California's State Capitol building, four bent straws under tinseled manes of brittle yellow plant rot. A squadron of dragonflies drift over their tops, almost evaporating into the sun's brilliance as they cross the ornate molding which yields the dome's rise, until the dragonflies hover to the statue of an Amerind on a rearing horse, his arm flexing wide to spear a marble bear.

And below, the man's lifeless eyes stay fixed in dissipation. He doesn't see visitors moving along the landmark. His head keeps nodding. His lips stammer on, the messages quietly coded in a rhythmic elusiveness that's only broken by the weight of a man sitting down on the bench. His sounds stop at once. His lips bind shut and his spine goes erect. He rises to his feet, slightly quaking. He launches into a quick walk on the north sidewalk, heading toward L Street and hurrying past the capitol's tall, gilded-age lamppost sopped in brown webs. He does not look back.

As soon as the mumbler blends into the shifting lines of foot traffic, three women dressed in pink come stepping up the same path. Today marks the one-year anniversary of the murder that altered Katie Tempesta's existence: She, Lynne Brown and her friend Ashlee are wearing Lisa's favorite color. Clasped in Katie's white, tensing fingers is a photo-laced urn holding her mother's ashes. One of the images within its leafed silver shows Lisa holding her infant granddaughter on Saint Patrick's Day. Lisa was always having impromptu family photos taken, and she could never pose enough with her granddaughter.

Now, a few reporters meet Katie on the west steps of the capitol.

Katie is here to talk about her mother, even though she knows the conversations happening in the halls behind her are focusing on anything but that: For weeks a tense showdown has been going on behind these walls. Despite the launching of

California's Realignment experiment, federal judges have ordered the department of corrections to lower its inmate population by five to six thousand individuals before the end of the year. For the first time in its history, California is staring down the barrel of an ordered mass prisoner release. With the 2013 legislative session coming to an end, Governor Jerry Brown quickly engineered a plan to transfer at least six thousand inmates to private, out-of-state prisons. Republican leadership backed the plan. Brown's own Democratic Party largely abandoned him, many unwilling to return to their constituents having voted for new dollars for more incarceration. The state senate's President pro Tempore Darrell Steinberg mustered a competing plan, one that would spend all new funds on substance abuse treatment and mental health services, taking a long-term preventative approach to the root issues of the prison overcrowding.

In the wake of the latest rulings from federal judges, Brown and Republican leaders accused Steinberg's group of willfully readying for a mass prisoner release. But Steinberg insisted the new investment in drug treatment and mental health would convince the inmate-plaintiffs to cease pressing for injunctive relief by the end of the year. In statements to reporters, Steinberg said the convicts' attorney Michael Bien was willing to urge federal judges to give California more time if lawmakers passed the new bill instead of their emergency incarceration plan. Brown and Republicans were quick to point out that it was now the federal judges—not Bien and his clients—in charge of whether there would be a mass release. Brown also expressed fears about putting the prisoner-plaintiffs, in his words, in charge of the state's correctional future. A showdown looked eminent.

Today, as Katie Tempesta stands yet again on the capitol's

marble steps, Governor Brown, Darrell Steinberg and the Assembly's Democrat and Republican leadership have announced a last-minute "compromise bill." The legislative maneuver will funnel an additional $750 million into prison-related substance abuse treatment and mental health services; but the spending boom is only guaranteed if federal judges extend their menacing deadline. Katie is preparing to speak to reporters at a moment when no one knows what the federal judges will do. If the judges refuse to ease pressure, then the new money in the bill shifts to being spent on private, corporate-owned prisons for about six thousand inmates.

Katie watches two microphones softly jab at her face. She is not here to talk about the legislative showdown going on inside the halls behind her, nor will she comment on the crafty theater of political posturing observed in the last week. Katie wants to talk about Realignment and PRCS, the strategies that were not enough to prevent a mass inmate release but were enough to play a role in the slaying of her mother.

"This is real," Katie insists to the reporters. "The crime is real. It happens to people, and it's happening more and more every day."

"So what's the answer?" a television personality fires back.

"I don't know," Katie replies. "But it's the state's job to figure it out—to do their job and take care of public safety." Keeping her glasses tight on her nose, Katie points to a photograph of her baby. "My daughter will never get to know her grandmother," she adds. "And it breaks my heart. My mother loved this little girl more than life itself."

The cameras power down. They drift away from Katie. And then the platoon of reporters walks off as Katie sets her mother's urn down on a marble slab. She and Lynne Brown have prepared a stack of letters to deliver to Governor Brown, Darrell Steinberg and a host of prominent lawmakers.

"We know we want to deliver these to the members of the Senate and Assembly safety committees," Lynne says, pulling the papers together. "And we're going to hand them over, out and open, not in envelopes, to make sure whoever takes them will have their eyes drawn to the first couple of lines."

"So that means we're bringing one up to Loni Hancock?" Katie asks, her thoughts dwelling on a woman she believes has been only cold and distant during their numerous encounters. Lynne nods. Katie reaches out for the envelopes. "I'll do it," she mutters. "I'll hand it to her myself."

The three pink-clad women get in line to pass through a metal detector guarding the capitol's hallways.

"I don't think they are going to let you through with the urn," Lynne whispers.

In an instant a trio of state police in dark suits and ties asks Katie to run all of her belongings through the scanner. Katie musters a tight, tense concentration—a librarian's poker face. "These are my mother's ashes," she explains, lifting the urn up.

A squinting pause runs from one officer's face to another. Wordless glances dart back and forth. A female officer steps closer, looking at the urn. Before she can formulate a question Katie starts talking again: "My mother was murdered by a PRCS offender, so I take her ashes with me whenever I go speak with legislators."

With eyes locked on the urn, the female officer lets a few soundless beats go by before saying, "Alright…just hand it to me as you go through."

Katie walks with a purpose, crossing straight through the chrome frame of the detector. She reaches down for her phone and purse, and then lifts her mother's ashes. Turning, her unbreakable focus shifts to a staircase that portals up to California's offices of power.

FOUR WEEKS BRING a honey glaze of fall staining the region's treetops, the winds stirring a mix of soft, flame-red leaves hardening on gold foliage and ever-whitening grass tips in the fields.

In Sacramento's neighboring city of Roseville, a police gang unit is attempting to monitor several members of the Sureños. It is three o'clock. The October sky is oddly warm. Roseville police officers Mike Ryland and Mike Sidebottom are perched in the front of an unmarked white Chevy truck. Sitting in the back seat is Homeland Security Special Agent R. Kennedy. The truck waits near the intersection of Sixth Street and B Street. And then an unexpected face comes into view: Sammy Duran sails by the team on a bicycle. Duran is a 32-year-old validated member of the Roseville Tiny Locos, a hyper-local subset of the Sureños. Of scant height and twiggy strength, Duran has facile cheeks under a wiredrawn, shaven head. Ryland knows Duran's thirteen-year history of getting arrested for battery, selling drugs, false imprisonment and resisting arrest. Probation records indicate he was high on methamphetamine during most of these episodes. In 2008, Duran was convicted of carjacking, fighting with police officers and bashing his own stepfather's skull with a hammer. The crime spree earned him five years in California's prison system. Several months ago, Duran took a drug test for his parole officer and came up positive for methamphetamine.

He vanished the next day.

Now Duran glides along Sixth Street on his bike, pedaling past two Roseville gang detectives and a U.S. immigration officer. The Chevy begins to roll. Ryland hits its flashing lights. Duran yanks his elbows on the handlebars to steer down Windsor Drive, aiming toward the home of his aunt Donna Sandoval. The Sureño's aunt and brother are inside the abode as he comes coasting through the carport. The Chevy pulls to a stop near Sandoval's driveway. All three officers watch Duran hurry behind a corner near the back of the house. Agent Kennedy climbs out of the Chevy, moving by a truck parked along the north wall. Ryland gets out to follow. Then Duran reappears, coming around the carport with both hands tightening on the grip of a .45-caliber pistol. Ryland's eyes scan from Duran's face to the gaseous glint of a muzzle flash.

At the same moment, Roseville's black-and-white police cruisers are rolling through quiet stretches of the city. They idle past the Old Hollywood blade of the Tower Theatre rising over faded downtown storefronts. They coast by plaster-sculpted fountains and fat Canary Island palm trees jammed around English facades of shopping centers. They breeze past trails on soft-sloped hills splashing toward the county's eastern orchards. And then each car—in concert—begins to slow.

"All units be advised," the dispatcher reports, "officer-involved shooting at 612 Windsor Drive. Officer down."

RYLAND AND SIDEBOTTOM hold defensive positions near the front of Donna Sandoval's house. Kennedy, dressed in jeans and a collared shirt under his tactical vest, watches a wet, ringed blood spot seeping through the denim over his leg. A Roseville police cruiser accelerates to the curb. Kennedy feels an officer grab him, helping him hobble to the patrol car's open door. The wounded agent drops down into the passenger seat. The patrol car speeds away.

More Roseville police units swoop in. With weapons drawn, a handful of officers make their way along the front yards of Windsor Drive. They survey the square lawns and flat ranch-style dwellings from the 1950s. Some of Duran's friends are trailing them from the far sidewalk. Benjamin Felix, a validated Sureño gang member, is videoing the officers with a cell phone. "Fucking pigs!" Felix taunts. "Look at these fucking pigs!" He notices a neighbor pointing out the direction Duran fled. "Fucking snitch boy!" Felix fumes, aiming his camera at the witness.

Roseville officer Kate Quartarolo approaches a low, chain-link fence running over pale flares of sedge. It is six minutes since backup arrived. Quartarolo nears the pickets of a barn-red fence on Windsor Drive, seeing a neighbor point down to a narrow run of dead leaves over a lawn. She spots Duran lying prone against the fence. The fugitive pounces up near the low lip of a bush. He starts to pull his semi-auto. Quartarolo moves first, drilling four shots at him.

Men and women walking on Sixth Street hit the ground. From the grit of the pavement, a few bystanders glimpse Duran charging their way. They watch him jump a five-foot fence, dead-dropping onto his face in the yard of a home on Hampton Drive. The impact blasts one of his shoes off—sends his cell phone skittering across the dirt.

Duran pushes himself up, bolting onto a porch and through an unlocked door. He still has his pistol. A man and women are inside as Duran races down their hallway. He dashes outside again, sprinting past a dull, purple-flaked Ford Fiesta. The Sureño crosses Hampton Drive before invading the side yard of a little white house. Four dogs hack a barking blitz at the screen door, and he hustles through an outer clutter of bikes, sandbox toys and garbage cans.

Sirens wail.

The running man jerks over a fence into a yard at Sixth Street and Mayfair Drive. He tries to penetrate another dwelling, though he can't pry open its lock nor can he see the homeowner staring out at him behind a set of blinds. He moves along the property and briefly hides his featherweight frame under a piece of plywood. He ducks out again, inching up to the front barrier of the fence at Mayfair: He can see police officers through its barred, wood-split lines.

More squad cars are coming to a stop along Sixth Street.

The next fence Duran capers over leads him to a sliding glass door of a house at Sixth Street and Hampton Drive. A young married couple, with a 15-month-old baby girl, listens as the wanted man enters. The family quickly barricades themselves in a nursery and Duran tries to force his way to them with his gun. He can't get into the room. He turns his attention back to the windows. Duran is cornered. The Roseville Police SWAT members are readying their 16,000-pound Bearcat armored truck to go through the side of the fence of 600 Hampton Drive. The sun hits its dull, flint-fern sides and coal-primer grill, flashing on two square windows above its hood that give the ballistic SUV the look of a steel, cubist bull.

Fitted in dark army gear, each team operative keeps near the Bearcat, checking his helmet and the action on his assault weapon. Among the eight-man crew are Dan Szeto, a popular patrol officer, Tyler Wolters, a longtime SWAT member, Scott Blynn, a former Sacramento sheriff's deputy who's worked dangerous gang areas, and Shad Begley, an officer known for his extreme physical fitness, as well as blasting 1950s Elvis music in his patrol car. The team is set. Neighbors peeking through their windows see the Bearcat go crashing through the high wooden planks of the fence, obliterating twenty-two feet of it into open space.

The SWAT members make a tactical entry into the yard.

A .45-caliber bullet—known by Sureños as a man-stopping "kill" round—flashes from an open window of the house.

POLICE ARE STILL securing the scene at Donna Sandoval's address. Roseville officer Carlos Cortes stands by a sheriff's deputy near a wall between Windsor Street and Riverside Avenue. Cortes can see a desultory row of faces gawking from behind the limp rope of a used car dealership across the empty boulevard. A static chirp clicks over his radio, briefly blinking into an analog hiss that gives way to a voice calling, "Shots fired! Shots fired!" Cortes tilts his head, dropping his ear close to the receiver on his shoulder. "Officers down!" the SWAT member yells. "Multiple men down! We've got an officer shot in the face!"

The center of Cortes' brow threads inward, a pushed, pinched tensing above his eyes, until his blunted expression slowly rises to meet the gaze of the deputy. Neither man utters a word.

"We need a route in," a Roseville firefighter breaks over the radio. "Can we bring units up Dudley?"

"Negative," a SWAT officer shouts. "Do not come up Dudley—he has a line of fire where Dudley meets Mayfair."

A HOMEOWNER ON Sixth Street braves a peek out her window. Nicknamed "the neighborhood pit bull" for how often she calls Roseville police, the woman has spent years getting to know different officers by name. Now, as roaring reports of the firefight dissolve on tree branches, she risks putting her face up by the glass. Her eyes instantly blanch with tears. She sees Tyler Wolters holding his Colt M-4 with one hand—its barrel glowing white from spitting thirty rounds—and using his free arm to drag Dan Szeto out of the razed hole in the fence. Shad Begley has his helmet off near a battery of patrol cars, a thick line of blood streaming down his forehead to his chin. Scott Blynn, who'd lead-lit Duran's position with twelve rounds from his M-4, catches his breath with the other SWAT operatives still on their feet. Down but breathing, Szeto is pulled to safety. Another armored vehicle drives in, along with a Roseville fire engine. Two officers rush a crash cart over to Szeto. His helmet is off as they hustle him to the back of an armored SUV.

Inside the house, the young couple and their infant barricaded in the nursery are still breathing. They had lain down when the storm of projectiles cut through the walls. Bullet holes warm in the doors, radiate in the walls, shell casings sit hot in the tray of the baby's highchair.

ONLOOKERS BEGIN TO congregate on lawns. A few edge up to the crime tape. They peer at a sheriff's K9 handler resting his hands on his knees while officers and deputies are checking rifles at his side. The state's Fugitive Apprehension

Team drives up: These newly arrived parole officers already know that Sammy Duran's crime spree has a link to California's Realignment law. Duran managed to serve less than the full five years for assaulting his stepfather with a hammer. He was back on the streets by December of 2012. Duran officially absconded from his parole supervision that same month. He was captured on April 15, 2013. The California Board of Prisons soon found him guilty of fugitive actions. Prior to Realignment, Duran could have been returned to a state penitentiary. However, Realignment now mandates that any prison convict coming back onto the streets who commits a technical parole violation—such as absconding—be punished with county jail time rather going back to state prison. Duran also benefited from the fact that Realignment dictates prison parolees dropped into county jails for violations receive automatic half-time chipped off their new sentences. In Duran's case, the California Board of Prisons sentenced him to one hundred days in the Placer County jail; yet with automatic half-time subtracted from his term, including the days already spent in custody, Duran was back on the streets four days after receiving his sentence. When state parole agents realized, weeks later, he was testing positive for methamphetamine use, his whereabouts were unknown.

Until now.

Neighbors continue to mass near the edge of the scene's western perimeter. In the maze of armor and aluminum, cops watching the house suddenly spot Duran trying to dash outside with his gun. Three Sacramento police officers and two West Sacramento officers punch the triggers of AR-15s, M-4s and .40-calibers. The residents on the street feel their spines harden. A crashing cadence of pop-chops booms under the birch branches. The drum line of cold thundering pushes on the tympanic membrane of every ear. Teeth clenched, bystanders can see the gun muzzles coughing, faintly flinching, their ejection ports arching the air with tiny geysers of up-jacked shells.

YEAR III

"All the time I hate what I am doing
and want the other. In a room full of people
I get frantic in their air…All you've
done is cut me in half, pointing me here.
Where I don't want these answers."

—Michael Ondaatje *Coming Through Slaughter*

CHAPTER 9

April, Dixon, Illinois: The Unseen

DIXON PRISON SUPERINTENDENT C.D. Eubanks approaches X-House, watching a chain of inmates ushered from its red scalpriform dimensions. Bare, leafless, harshly cut trees rise off a nearby lawn. Eight years after the hostage crisis, X-House continues to be Dixon's maximum-security wing for the most dangerous psychotic and schizophrenic inmates in Illinois. These are the prisoners that pass by Eubanks now, tramping aimlessly, ranging idly, a lined kennel of jeans and perfect blue shirts. Some make eye contact with the superintendent. Others peer south to the glint-crescents that flinch on razor wire bridling the fence: Cold Christmas lights of blades and reflections.

It is Dixon's first sunny morning in days. Approaching the door, Eubanks sees an inmate stop and pivot. He steps out of the shuffling channel. He's a tall white man with smoky, wild hair. His beard flows down in hispid wires. Eubanks does not look closely at him yet; but the journalist trailing behind does, seeing a profane erraticism lit in the inmate's eyes. "There you are," the man snarls. "I told you—"

Eubanks, wearing slacks, a button-down shirt and windbreaker, shows no reaction when the prisoner steps toward him.

"I told you!" the inmate repeats in a seething grunt.

"What?" Eubanks asks flatly. The superintendent will not avert his eyes to the officer at his left, nor will he glance to the X-House portal where a sergeant waits past the doorway. Instead Eubanks steps face-to-face with the mountain's crashed expression.

"You!" the inmate gnarrs again.

Eubanks taps his belt, lifts his chest under the dress shirt and drops his chin: His eyes cut into the other man's aberrant gaze. "You need to fall back in line," Eubanks tells him.

The prisoner gawps hard, and Eubanks returns a stare, with an eyebrow hoisted, until the inmate's elephantine frame lumbers back into the moving line of denim. The men push on toward the white columns and classic brick arches of the next cellblock.

Eubanks steps into X-House with the journalist keeping up at his side. If the superintendent had been attacked seconds before he could have had twenty correctional officers running with an "all call" over the radio. That means it's a decent year. Both the prison's warden, Nedra Chandler, and the Illinois correctional officers' union have spoken publicly about fluctuating employee ratios since the standoff that made Dixon a headline news story. Regardless of what the inmate-to-officer ratio is during a given month, every man and woman working at Dixon knows staff never have as much security as they want. While the same holds true for resources within the prison's mental health wing, Eubanks and his crew have worked to increase the level of treatment services: X-House and the other units in its division may be holding inmates who have committed crimes ranging from assault to murder, but the glaring truth is that ninety-eight percent of them are serving sentences of twenty years or less. Most will parole. Treating their psychosis is more than a safety or civil rights issue—it is an obligation to guard the neighborhoods they will eventually be returning to.

Eubanks now has a team with expertise in managed patient care, emergency care and crisis intervention. He has recruited correctional officers who will partner with psychiatrists, psychologists and social workers assigned to individual inmates. Staff is engaged in a constant cycle of assessing. Eubanks pushes to have the status of thirty to forty mentally ill prisoners reviewed every week. He and Chandler call the process "full intervention." The John Howard Association—the watchdog group so critical of most of Illinois's prisons—recently conducted an independent tour of Dixon and gave it a generally positive report, including its mental health division.

JHA inspectors did, however, note mental health workers at Dixon "expressed that they could use three times the number of staff."

For now Eubanks has to work with the employee count the Illinois legislature has budgeted for him. Perfect, imagined scenarios are of little use. Passing the maroon-colored cell doors, Eubanks reviews the complicated factors at play when it comes to a number of the inmates' prognoses. One challenge involves taking reasonable steps to protect mentally ill inmates from further trauma resulting from sexual and physical violence. The issue is paramount in the majority of Dixon's medium-security cells outside of X-House. At this moment one of Eubanks' lieutenants is reviewing files on inmates being transferred in, attempting to identify "vulnerables." The key is knowing who the "vulnerables" are, and then to avoid celling them with sophisticated, violent or predatory prisoners.

"I'm not going to stick an eighteen or nineteen-year-old in the same cell as an inmate in his forties or fifties," Eubanks reflects. "There are certain people who have been in here long enough to know what situations they can take advantage of—and so we try to not put them in a position to do that."

Gang reunification is another circumstance that causes problems within the housing units, including tension and bloodshed that can interfere with the treatment of multiple inmates. Dixon's officers review which cellblocks and housing units known gang members are celled in, and stay vigilant for offenders trying to subtly take authority of areas of the prison, whether through intimidation, manipulation or force of personality. If Eubanks learns of specific inmates exerting influence over a block, he personally issues a warning or will order the convict re-celled.

"One thing I can say, at least about our facility, is that no one runs this prison but us," Eubanks affirms.

Yet overhauling Dixon's wirescape of brick and steel does not guarantee safety from its clouded minds. Eubanks ushers his journalist guest down the same hallways of X-House where the hostage-taking unfolded years before and, walking along a cell door, a scalded grating voice calls in a hurting half-cough through its window. The throat's brazen bark stops the two men: Its syllables are lacerated with urgent certainty.

"What did he say?" the reporter asks.

Pausing, Eubank's brow lifts, "He said, 'I've got magic.'"

Records from the Illinois Department of Corrections list more than eleven thousand inmates as requiring mental health services, with four thousand deemed "seriously mentally ill." According to California's Department of Corrections, thirty percent of The Golden State's offenders are classified as mentally ill, equating to one hundred-and-thirty-five thousand inmates. In 2010, a study co-sponsored by the National Sheriffs' Association found that, in Louisiana, for every mentally ill citizen receiving in-patient treatment there were five mentally ill people being housed in jails or prisons.

At Dixon Correctional Center, prisoners lost in the realms of schizophrenia or psychotic wandering can be difficult to reach.

"Inmates have the right to refuse treatment," Warden Chandler explains. "That's something I don't think the public always knows. There are times we can intervene, if an inmate is suicidal or a threat to himself; but if they're not, a mentally ill patient can refuse treatment—and they have that right."

She adds, "When it comes to handling those kind of offenders, it's day-to-day in here."

And some of those days still include paroling mentally ill convicts. Counselors at Dixon have a multi-tiered strategy to attempt easing these inmates back into their communities. They assist offenders in getting forms of identification, which are critical to obtaining health care services, including birth certificates, social security cards and copies of driver's licenses. Illinois' parole re-entry group helps prisoners search for housing options. Dixon's psychiatric team gives mentally unstable men being released a two-week supply of their medication, as well as a prescription for another two weeks. They also issue instructions on how to use the new federal Affordable Care Act and various other programs to get their meds.

However, while the staff at Dixon Correctional Center keeps working on tactics to get the best result for mentally ill inmates, a central irony now resonates in the fact its overhauled services often will not be matched by the Illinois counties those offenders are paroled back to. According to the National Alliance on Mental Illness, since the onset of the Great Recession the State of Illinois has cut its mental health budget by $187 million—a thirty-one percent decrease: California made similar cuts, while Alabama slashed its own spending on the mentally ill by nearly forty percent. Such cuts were not entirely welded to the Recession. Data from the Illinois Hospital Association indicates that, over the last sixty years, the number of state-run psychiatric hospital beds in Illinois decreased from thirty-five thousand to fourteen hundred. The same report indicates that Illinois currently has more than fifty counties with no licensed psychiatrist at all, and another fourteen staffed with only one for its entire population.

These are the same communities the inmates from Dixon's mental health division will be paroled back into.

On this sunny afternoon, as Nedra Chandler works in her modest office under the century-old cupola, and C.D. Eubanks inspects the concrete floors of X-House, many members of Illinois's department of corrections are still thinking about a hearing which happened in Washington, D.C. three weeks ago: One of the key witnesses was Thomas Dart, the sheriff of Illinois' largest county.

Dart's testimony was before the United States House of Representatives' Energy and Commerce Committee's subcommittee for oversight and investigation. The topic was violent crime perpetrated by those suffering from intense, untreated mental illness. Congressman Tim Murphy opened the hearing up by reviewing six different mass-causality shooting incidents in U.S. neighborhoods in the last seven years.

"All (of the shooters) exhibited a record of untreated, severe mental illness prior to their crimes," Murphy observed. "It is a reflection of the total dysfunction of our current mental health system that, despite clear warning signs, these individuals failed to receive in-patient or out-patient treatment for their illnesses, that might have averted these tragedies. And they all leave us wondering, 'What would have happened, if?'... Part of the problem is that our laws on involuntary commitment are in dire need of modernization. It is simply unreasonable, if not a danger to public safety, that our current system often waits until an individual is on the brink of harming himself, or others, or has already done so, before any action can be taken."

Five witnesses into the proceedings, Sheriff Dart was called on to testify. The jail Dart operates in Cook County has become one of the largest mental health care treatment facilities in the nation. Cook County—with Chicago as its center—has a daily inmate population of ten to twelve-thousand men and women. On any given day, Dart told the committee, between thirty to thirty-five percent of those inmates and detainees have an acute, diagnosable mental illness.

"Since becoming sheriff in 2006, I have seen an explosion of seriously mentally ill individuals housed in the jail," Dart said into his microphone. "I have seen first-hand the devastating impact cuts to mental health programs and services have to the mentally ill in Illinois...I find it ironic that in the 1950s we thought it inhumane to house people in state hospitals, but now, in the 21st century, we're OK with them being housed in jails."

To demonstrate the monetary and operational confusion his staff is witnessing, Dart reviewed the recent stories of three mentally ill suspects in the Cook County Jail. The first was a man the sheriff referred to as "J.J.," an arrestee who had been off his medications when he shoplifted a few sheets and towels from a Walgreens drugstore. Mumbling on his way out, J.J. asked cashiers to "charge" the fabrics to an imaginary credit card he may have thought was real.

J.J. then spent one-hundred and ten days in jail before he was sentenced to probation. Dart did the math for the subcommittee. "The taxpayers of Cook County spent close to $16,000 after a failed attempt to steal $29.99 worth of merchandise from Walgreens," the sheriff observed.

Dart's next story was more disturbing. He mentioned "J.D.," a Chicago-area resident diagnosed with a psychotic disorder that makes him experience shuddering visions. The Cook's County Sheriff's Office was trying to execute a local warrant for J.D. when he was apprehended out-of-state in California. While sitting in a California jail, J.D.'s mental mirages became too terrifying and he stopped them by ripping out one of his own eyeballs.

Sheriff Dart made it clear to the committee that the sickening saga was not over.

"He was transferred to our custody two weeks ago and recently attempted to remove his remaining eye," Dart said. "My staff acted quickly, and we are hopeful his sight can be restored."

Dart's final example involved a woman he referred to as "T.A.," a disordered personality his deputies had arrested more than a hundred times. The sheriff recalled that T.A.'s latest run-in with the law involved stealing $20 from a purse during a church service. Dart's jail personnel were immediately confronted with the nightmare of how T.A.'s mental illness manifests itself when she's in custody. Classified as "a chronic self-mutilator," T.A. spends her time in cells tearing her own arms to throbbing flesh pulp with her fingernails. During her last arrest, Dart's team was forced to fit her with special mittens that went all the way up to her armpits.

Before concluding his remarks, the sheriff ran through a host of new programs his department implemented to deal with mentally ill individuals pinging in and out of the Cook County Jail: The strategies included improved communication with prosecutors, public defenders and the patients' family members. Dart's office is also funding its own twenty-four-hour mental health crisis line. But the sheriff made it clear that he and other local law enforcement administrators are fighting a rearguard action.

"We are in an unsustainable position," Dart emphasized. "Every day I am faced with the mental health crisis in the county, and in this country."

While the sheriff's testimony was given to members of Congress, the federal government's role in mental health services has been minimal for three decades and running. The Omnibus Budget Recognition Act of 1981 repealed the national Mental Health Systems Act, effectively reducing Washington, D.C.'s commitment to mental health care to the role of being a simple distributor of direct block grants to individual states. Those block grants have been gradually but substantially reduced since the passing of the Omnibus Act.

With federal and state funds sliding, local leaders across

Illinois have decisions to make: Counties, cities and townships within Illinois have the authority to create their own 708 Mental Health Boards, which can levy local taxes for the mission of funding augmented mental health services. Yet, as Dart settles back in Cook County from his trip to Washington, D.C., and C.D. Eubanks walks through the echoing voices of X-House, and Warden Chandler reviews reports and staffing levels, the hope of individual counties across the state getting more involved in mental health services is not encouraging: Only twenty-seven of the one-hundred-and-two counties in Illinois are currently operating their own 708 Mental Health Boards. Knowing how many counties are not getting involved in the crisis is a reality that correctional officers, doctors and administrators of Dixon Correctional Center have a hard time ignoring, especially when they circle back to the statistic that ninety-eight percent of their mentally ill inmates will ultimately be paroled.

"The challenge is getting inmates that continuum of care once they're released," Chandler points out. "A lot of counties in Illinois tend to look at behavioral health services as discretionary spending…if parolees who are mentally ill don't have families making sure they get their meds and doctors appointments, then the odds of re-offending can be high."

CHAPTER 10

Return to Slaughter

GERALD METHVIN FEELS the balmy Louisiana afternoon strafed by a breeze. Cool currents rush by, grinding the mantis-colored grass on pastures beyond his mobile home park. A low-sitting warmth collides with new air. Methvin tightens down on the handlebars of his ride-on lawn mower, accelerating past the horse corral as curling dust whips off pale, brown gravel. He notices a Lincoln MKS rolling into the park's entrance off Highway 67. The car slowly circles a line of double-wides and then stops in front of an empty unit. That same desolate lot number is always on Methvin's mind. The Lincoln parks near the graying, unpainted wood steps tilted up against its aluminum siding. Methvin knows that if this stranger knocks he will find no one behind the broken, dangling blinds. There has been a lot of trouble for Methvin around that mobile. It has some special meanings for him now, and one of those insights is that the Devil knows exactly who to reach for.

The moment that shook the town of Slaughter came on an August evening around 5 p.m.

Marie Smothers, age eighty-seven, had lived in the Country Breeze Park for nearly a decade. But life was different for her now: For the last three weeks she had been caring for an 8-year-old boy who'd just come to stay with her. Smothers' neighbors still have some confusion about whether the child was her great-grandson or great-grandnephew. They do know he was hers to raise for the moment, and he called her grandma. Quiet and polite, Smothers was rarely seen outside of her unit, except for when she occasionally asked the young woman next door for help with the garbage. As owner of the Country Breeze, Methvin and his family considered her loyal to a fault. They and others who lived in the park suspected she was giving what little money she had to family members who were chronically struggling. Methvin would watch occasional strangers pull up, walking along the magenta vine-stems that sprouted up against loosened pieces of skirting around her trailer's bottom.

Now the same impulse that had driven Smothers to help her kin led her to serve as the primary caregiver for an 8-year-old. Smothers' neighbors were off-put by the situation: The boy was too little and petite to care for Smothers, and, likewise, the elderly woman was nearly an invalid and hardly prepared to be a parent again. East Feliciana Parish's elementary school was due to start in a few weeks; but neighbors worried that the boy would only be going if he chose to, as there was no one in Smothers's home who could make him go—or do anything if he didn't want to.

According to the parish sheriff's department, the boy was quickly contacted by law enforcement after he called 911 and said someone was trying to kill him. When deputies arrived the boy admitted the call was a prank. He was warned about the seriousness of making false reports.

And then came the noise. Gerald Methvin was not outside

when the cracking static-roar went out. But a woman staying two units down from Smothers' trailer heard it. "What was that?" she asked, turning to her sister. Fifteen minutes later, the boy appeared on the gravel road, pleading for help. Neighbors thought they heard him say, "Someone has shot my grandmother." Others believed he simply said, "Grandma's asleep."

A nurse and two other women from the park went through Smothers' front door. They found her sitting in an easy chair. She was slumped over with a splotch of blood on her shoulder. The nurse turned Smothers' head and a gored opening flashed from in her skull. The boy started crying and ran over to his uncle's unit on the back end of the mobile home park.

East Feliciana Parish District Attorney Sam D'Aquilla soon pulled into Country Breeze to find a battery of sheriff's cruisers in front of Smothers' trailer and a crowd of onlookers waiting on the other side of the crime tape. Moving through the little dwelling's narrow tunnel, D'Aquilla and homicide detectives took in the details of the scene. There was an entrance wound from a Colt .38-caliber in the back of the old woman's head, but no exit hole from the front of her face. They noticed a screen-saver bouncing on the monitor of a computer near the small, four-burner stove. A deputy reached over and flicked its mouse. The screen came aglow with the menu for Grand Theft Auto IV, a video game which allows players to ambush and kill police officers, murder prostitutes in cold blood and run over pedestrians while wasted behind the wheel. Some of the player's shooting victims scream for help while the game's main character taunts them.

Media agencies were beginning to swarm outside of

Smothers' mobile. With no obvious motive for the killing, sheriff's officials decided to acknowledge that it appeared the 8-year-old was playing Grand Theft Auto IV just minutes before walking up behind Smothers, pointing the gun at her and pulling the trigger.

A WIND BATS against Methvin's overalls, touching his weathered work shirt and the crumpled colorless flat cap pulled over his steely hair. Behind him a horse trots through the clement breath under the cloud cover, its hooves kicking dirt up along the chipped, silver planks of an aged barn. Marie Smothers' death brought reporters from all over the nation to Methvin's quiet piece of Louisiana. A week after the coroner left, Methvin's son, Glen, was driving his truck through the dark morning hours on the highway when he heard a radio talk show from New York mentioning his parents' little mobile home park. The last time Methvin remembers a platoon of cameramen invading the parish was when he helped crews from Oliver Stone's film "JFK" scout locations and vintage cars between Slaughter and Angola.

If only the Feliciana parishes' fame could have ended there. Yet History runs deep through the June Bug shimmer of darker treetops in its greenways, binding meadows and Spanish moss to an earlier story entwined in the community's memory: Thirteen miles north of Methvin's mobile home park stands a building known for most of its existence as the Louisiana State Insane Asylum. The titan's Pantheon-like pillars have hosted the evolution of psychiatric treatment for more than a century and a half; and before that timeline's midway mark it was the final requiem of disintegration for the New Orleans trumpeter who blew the first notes of a new era. Though a multitude of souls expired in the asylum, the midnight-minded coronet player Buddy Bolden represents the most American and anti-American of narratives—a man from a poor, racially segregated neighborhood whose creative conjuring and manic energy fused the diverse echoes of a nation into an endless bridge of artistry, a launching point for other musicians to spiritually elevate the world, even after Bolden himself withdrew into the shroud of mental illness, locked away, left alone, buried in a pauper's grave and then all but forgotten.

The old asylum still towers. East Feliciana Parish watched the brick megalith rise on an outer field between 1848 and 1853. The rail lines had rocked with freight cars laden in sash pulleys, weights, lime, cement, slating, posts, copper, tin, iron, caps, bases, glass sculptures and massive marble mantels: When construction ended neighbors were staring at one of the most looming feats of Greek Revival architecture in the deep South.

Records show that the Louisiana State Insane Asylum opened its doors in 1857 to five hundred and eighty-seven incoming patients. They wandered up rutted mud in wagon train processions, sitting in crowded, subdued clusters on buckboards as the horses trudged up to the superstructure. The most common diagnoses made that year were dementia, "moral" problems, monomania and idiocy. Melancholia and mania were also valid conditions for admittance. Of the entire first class of patients, only one was listed as "homicidal." The vast majority of these men and women came from the bustling port community of Orleans Parish. The Crescent City's growing, up-river neighborhoods of Jefferson Parish provided the second-highest number, tied only by—ironically—the quiet, rural hamlet of East Feliciana Parish itself. While the most common professions of the incoming patients were laborers and servants, records show in its inaugural year the asylum could boast having at least one clergyman, one rabbi, one type-setter and one "circus rider."

The first chief physician to work with the institute's patients was acutely aware of the social conditions they had been immersed in before coming to him.

"My tabular statement of the various forms of insanity manifested here will show that the amount of dementia is, relatively, very great," Dr. J.E.T. Gourlay wrote to the facility's board of directors in 1857. "It much exceeds the average in other insane asylums, and the fact is probably owing to the presence in this institution of an undue portion of individuals previously subjected to a career of hardship, sickness and destitution."

On June 5, 1907 a man who was famous in the Uptown neighborhoods of New Orleans arrived at the asylum's segregated dormitory. The previous summer Charles "Buddy" Bolden had been the king of dance halls and saloons from the west Mississippi banks of Algiers to the red light district of Storyville. Bolden was the first band leader to fuse the brass power-punch of parade music with the energy of ragtime, and then, through emotionally liberated improvisation, coat the sound with a suffering edge of "the hard blues" drifting off the river docks. He was never recorded during his life but his burning brand of "low-down music" would be remembered in Uptown New Orleans. Louis Armstrong would tell stories of walking along Perdido Street as a child and seeing Bolden "blow so hard" on his trumpet the image lingered with intoxicating awe. The pathfinder pianist Jelly Roll Morton would famously remember Bolden as "the most blowingest man since Gabriel." Other groundbreaking performers, including the trombonist Kid Ory and trumpeter Bunk Johnson, would also look back on Bolden as the human lightning rod that sparked the musical kinesis known as jazz.

At the height of Bolden's brief fame his band mates and fans suddenly witnessed an alarming transformation in him. He was overtaken with unexplained fits of rage followed by obsessive spells of paranoia. He had trouble recognizing people he had known for years on the street. Unexplained headaches morphed into fleeting mirages of the mind. During the New Orleans Labor Day parade in 1906, Bolden was blasting his trumpet in a marching band when something—according to local memory—snapped in his lucidity. Bolden fell out of the parade, disappearing from the crowd. He was 26-years-old. He would never perform again.

In May of 1907, a New Orleans judge signed an official declaration of insanity on Bolden, who was then transported to the asylum. Medical records document that Bolden spent the next twenty-four years calmly complying with the hospital's staff as he wandered around picking paint off the walls and silently touching random objects in the hallways. He was still a patient in East Feliciana Parish when he died in 1931. No obituary was ever published for him. Six family members attended his funeral at Holt Cemetery in New Orleans.

By World War II jazz had become the sonic psyche of young America. It was only then that journalists began to listen to older musicians reminiscing about King Bolden "bringing the whole street with him" when he would parade. In the early

1960s a researcher named Donald M. Marquis started trekking through Uptown New Orleans to interview elderly survivors who had actually known Bolden. When Marquis asked about the band leader's infamous breakdown, he was confronted with the mystery of full-tilt myth: Rumors abounded Bolden had been the target of Voodoo curses from scorned women; or that a poison had been dabbed on the mouthpiece of his trumpet; or that he'd smashed his own brains by blowing his horn too loud. A decade after Marquis noted these stories, the novelist Michael Ondaatje began to chase Bolden's ghost up Liberty Street, after becoming obsessed with a single sentence echoing from Storyville—"Buddy Bolden, who became a legend when he went berserk in a parade." Ondaatje went on to write the haunting meditation "Coming Through Slaughter" about the trumpeter. The novel's final pages touch on warnings from the Baptist Church that Bolden spent his early life in: "Some say you went mad by trying to play the Devil's music and hymns at the same time."

But all of these catechisms and innuendos simply demonstrate the power of the human imagination to poetically deflect uncomfortable truths. Existing records of one of Bolden's medical evaluations from 1927 make it clear his unraveling was not born from playing demonic brass notes, nor was it inflicted on him by Afro-Caribbean curses. The asylum doctors wrote that Bolden suffered from paranoid delusions, auditory and visual hallucinations and grandiose confusion. "Insight and judgment lacking," his doctor observed. "Has a string of talk that is incoherent. Hears the voices of people that bothered him before he came here."

Buddy Bolden was mentally ill. The chemistry and function

of his brain had faltered. In conjunction with the expectations linked to mental illness during his lifetime, Bolden was locked away and hidden from the public. In concert with the era's codes on race and poverty, when he died he was loaded on a train and hauled to a pauper's cemetery in New Orleans for burial in an unmarked grave. The "first man of jazz" may have changed the musical language of the world; but the grasp of mental illness on him merged with broader legacies of indigence and indifference to make him totally disposable. The title of Ondaatje's book emphasized the end of that journey, reimagining the train carrying Bolden's cheap, wooden coffin as it cut straight through the town of Slaughter before rolling on for the murky, tangled swamps to the south.

Today, the old train tracks still cleave through the center of Slaughter, running hen-speckled and empty over gouged lagoons of grass, past a cottage with its lax spray of vines hanging from ruptured boards, and then straight along the wood structures with tin hats blotted in carrot-blood corrosion, and still on, under the ascending eggshell of a water tower with the blue, stenciled letters of S L A U G H T E R punctuated across its corniform.

And behind those tracks, hidden from Highway 10 by a span of trees, the asylum still functions as a treatment center of the mentally ill, under its modernized name of the East Louisiana State Hospital. The five hundred-bed facility has a host of doctors and nurses providing psychiatric screenings, consultations and outpatient treatment. It also has a forensic unit for housing prisoners who committed crimes but were found technically not guilty by reason of insanity. The hospital is a refuge for troubled minds, though lately it has been increasingly isolated in Louisiana. Federal and state budget cuts recently compelled officials to downsize and privatize Southeast Louisiana Hospital in Mandeville. The move was made despite the institute's glowing reports on performance and care from independent commissions. The southeast hospital's change was part of a rapid succession of blows to mental health care in Louisiana, which included shuttering the psychiatric wing of Charity Hospital in New Orleans and a temporary four-year closure of New Orleans Adolescent Hospital. Now, East Louisiana Hospital and its sister facility in Pineville are the only large treatment centers left, and both have been hit with direct budget reductions.

From the vantage point of the National Alliance on Mental Illness, the downsizing of services in Louisiana has had an impact on the state's crowded jails and prisons. Nichole McGee is the executive director of NAMI's Louisiana division, and she gets continual feedback from her organization's chapters in different parishes— reports on example after example of diagnosable mentally ill individuals being arrested for crimes that might have been prevented with medication or treatment.

"That's something we're hearing about in different parts of Louisiana, and right here in our own backyard in Baton Rouge," McGee says. "One strategy we've been working on involves trying to get Crisis Intervention Team training for police and other members of law enforcement. It is training that helps indentify and handle people who are going through a mental health crisis, so those officers will know, and they'll react completely differently from the very start of a situation."

While those working with the mentally ill continue to pressure Louisiana lawmakers to fund CIT training, the broader spectrum of resources across the South remains bleak. And the challenges are coming home to the East Louisiana State Hospital. A fresh lawsuit from the Advocacy Center in New Orleans alleges that the institute's forensic unit for prisoner-patients is so full that multiple inmates who were ordered by judges to get treatment there—those found not guilty by reason of insanity— are now receiving little or no attention as they sit on a waiting list controlled by the Secretary of the Louisiana Department of Health and Hospitals.

The Antebellum asylum that Buddy Bolden once wandered through has stairwells and hallways that are little more than a museum, but the institute's guarded cellblocks have never been more full.

THE NATIONAL MEDIA'S fascination with Smothers' murder ended in three days. Over the next week newspaper reporters from Baton Rouge penned follow-up pieces before the story evaporated from the news cycle in Louisiana. The saga quietly became the property of prosecutors, defense attorneys and doctors working in East Feliciana Parish. For District Attorney Sam D'Aquilla, state law was clear that the 8-year-old suspect was too young to face prosecution.

"Under Louisiana law, if you're under ten years of age, you can't fit the requisite for having criminal thought," he explains. "That line has to start somewhere, and the legislature decided someone that young is not capable of criminal intent...I think there is just too much evidence the brain is not fully developed."

D'Aquilla used his authority to make sure the boy was put under the supervision of the department of family services, which would get him a long-term counselor to oversee various court-ordered therapy sessions. The child's juvenile status prevents D'Aquilla from speaking in-depth about the living situation he was ultimately put in, though the district attorney is confident psychologists will delve into whatever difficulties the boy was experiencing leading up to the homicide.

"Honestly, the counseling is not really about getting into his culpability," the prosecutor says. "They're just concerned with getting him the help he needs, so he can cope with what has happened. He killed someone who was close to him, and that is something that will follow him for the rest of his life. That's why he'll need counseling, and why it's important to get him the right kind…There's not much else you can say, other than it was just a tragic event."

The brief burst of media spotlight on the case was hyper-focused on the detail of an 8-year-old playing Grand Theft Auto IV just before the shooting. D'Aquilla does not think children should play Grand Theft Auto, and while he remains concerned about the possible effects it had on the boy, as an investigator he cannot say with clinical certainty it played a direct role in the homicide. But the journalism world was asking the question: Could daily mind-melting interactions with a digital stage of crime and cruelty account for the vision of a second-grader killing an elderly woman?

It is a query the U.S. scientific community is fiercely debating. In 2011, Dr. Vincent Matthews of Indiana University used structured, long-term M.R.I. brain scans on young men playing violent video games and compared them to ones who were not. Matthews' study indicated the young men playing violent video games showed less activity in the areas of the brain that involved "emotions, attention and inhibition of our impulses." Two years later, in the wake of the mass-casualty shooting at Sandy Hook Elementary School in Connecticut, forensic psychiatrists Vasilis Pozios, Praveen Kambam and H. Eric Bender published a joint op-ed in *The New York Times* that argued a meta-analysis of nearly all scientific studies between 1957 and 2014 paint a picture of a moderate-to-strong link between violent media exposure and violent behavior. In their op-ed, the forensic psychiatrists pointed out the Surgeon General, the National Institute of Mental Health, the American Medical Association and the American Psychiatric Association all consider media violence exposure a risk factor for actual violence.

Even as Sam D'Aquilla moves between his office and the stately white colonnades of the parish courthouse, a new *Time Magazine* article by Alice Parks highlights the latest study by Iowa State University on the nexus between brutal video games and disturbing behavior in grade school children. The study suggests that violent video games urge kids to act in more aggressive ways, with the number of hours played directly correlating to their heightened hostility. But with ninety-one percent of American children and teenagers playing video games, by some estimates, the Iowa State report had its critics. One of them was psychologist Christopher Ferguson of Stetson University, who pointed out to *Time* that "the rise in popularity of video gaming has not been matched by a similar rise in violent crime." Ferguson also raised a broader concern that, by putting so much emphasis on questionable video games, the medical community was losing sight of the direct stressors that fuel aggression in children and teens, such as violence in the home, forms of abuse and mental illness.

And for all of the studies being done on games like Grand Theft Auto, social workers and counselors across the U.S. are just as aware of a report published in 2012 in the peer-reviewed *PLOS ONE Journal*, in which psychiatric researchers at Dartmouth Medical School and Brown University found that early life stress, lack of parental nurturing, childhood abuse and abandonment are all associated—via the biochemistry of the brain— with increased risks for mental disorders.

"These findings suggest that childhood maltreatment or adversity may lead to epigenetic modifications of the human GR gene," the doctors wrote in their conclusions. "Alterations in methylation of this gene could underlie the associations between childhood adversity, alterations in stress reactivity, and risk for psychopathology."

Thuggish video games may be raising questions about American culture but the *PLOS ONE* findings touch on a different phenomenon—the point where cultures of crime and cultures of hopelessness intersect with a sustained culture of silence. According to the Children's Defense Fund, an organization founded in 1973 by members of the NAACP, Louisiana currently has over a quarter of a million children living in poverty, and every sixty-three minutes a child is abused or neglected in the state. Roughly five thousand children are circulating through Louisiana's foster care system, and the state has more than sixty-five thousand grandparents raising their grandchildren. The group Prevent Child Abuse Louisiana, the largest nonprofit of its kind in the state, cites studies linking as much as two-thirds of all child maltreatment cases directly to substance abuse. Public debate is still raging on whether drug addiction is a form of mental illness, but the scientific findings on how addiction's harvest of suffering can cause mental illness in children appears to be getting clearer by the day; and it is a story that has not brought an army of national reporters to East Louisiana Parish, nor any other struggling community in the South.

GERALD METHVIN WATCHES the white Lincoln back away from Marie Smothers' unit. He's wondering if he should pull his ride-on lawnmower in front of the car, stopping the stranger to see why he peered through the dead woman's sliding glass door. Even though Methvin and his wife Dot have been dealing with ongoing legal issues around trying to get Smothers' abandoned mobile home removed, the most disheartening aspect of glancing at that sliver of the park is the loss of one of their best tenants, a woman who was committed through personality and actions to the warm, peaceful, neighborly atmosphere the Methvins have striven to have at the Country Breeze. These days over half of the renters are bachelors needing part-time crash pads as they work at the oil refineries scattered near Baton Rouge. These men pass through East Feliciana Parish like ghosts. Smothers was quietly part of the scene, a piece of the communal fabric. Moreover, she was a woman who seemed to value family above all else, and that is conviction Methvin and his wife truly identify with.

Methvin swings his lawnmower out wide in front of the entrance to Highway 67, advancing with a rev up alongside of the Lincoln.

"You mind telling me why you're looking around that particular unit," he asks through the sedan's open driver's window.

"I'm a journalist," the man responds. "I'm following up on Miss Smothers' case."

"Alright," Methvin says, turning the lawnmower off. "Take a walk with me on over to the house."

Inside the cozy orbit of a living room he's called home for twenty-seven years, Methvin settles down into his easy chair, pushing his flat cap halfway up his scalp as he wipes his brow. Dot offers the stranger a drink. "Miss Smothers was a wonderful tenant," Methvin utters. "Never a problem. Never. I'll tell you, if I had ten more tenants like her," he adds, shaking his head.

Methvin talks a little about how the parish has changed over the years. Methamphetamine, pill addictions and burglaries are all common to read about in the local paper. He's called the sheriff's department himself on one tenant who was breaking into cars in the park. But, all things considered, life in the Country Breeze—life in Slaughter—had been fairly tranquil until the moment that .38-caliber sparked inside Smothers' trailer.

"The ingredients of the woman who got killed were what was lost in the news stories," Methvin says with a rough sigh. "No one values that anymore."

And since the flashing lights illuminated the Country Breeze on that terrible August evening, Methvin has contemplated values more than ever. He won't allow rap or hip-hop music to be blasted in the park if he hears a hint of violence against women. The bombardment of vicious images and virtual pathways of experience that a game like Grand Theft Auto IV offers doubly disturb him. By his way of thinking, in a landscape where addiction is common, child abandonment frequent and mental health services low, the broader American trend of allowing media play to dominate children's lives can have dire consequences.

"I get frustrated by how parents ruin these kids with sensationalism," Methvin says from his chair. "People have to steer away from it. These movies and video games have a strong influence on young people. When you quit teaching a child the best way to live, then it's going to be natural for them to want to be like what they see."

Leaning forward, his eyes heavy, he adds, "especially these little kids who are basically by themselves. As a Christian, it's hard to look at it any other way than the Devil knows who's really alone."

EPILOGUE

December, Folsom, California: Continuum

ROGER ANDERSON GLANCES at a leaden pyramid of bricks standing where oak woodlands meet an empty road. Plump, plated letters run in ebony across its altar: Folsom State Prison. The rear windshield frames a view of dappled granite and rocked towers—that old penitentiary Johnny Cash made famous with his concert in 1968. Roger had been an inmate there when director James Mangold arrived to film scenes for his telling of Cash's life, "Walk the Line." That was Roger's second stint at Folsom. Now, as his mother's car makes the turn from 300 Prison Road onto East Natoma Street, Roger is saying goodbye to his third stay at America's best-known bastion of incarceration. And it has not been Cash's "Folsom Prison Blues" echoing in his head these last months, but as always, the digging wire-ache of George Jones' voice, with its hard barbed silk straining through reverb and Marlboro smoke. "Still doing time."

The third year of California's Realignment experiment coincided with a banner period of suffering for the man called Country. After being arrested in Paloma, and then trying to kill himself in Jenny Lind, he was taken to jail months later, again, for possession of methamphetamine. Gabriel Lozano had claimed the meth inside the Paloma house, leaving Roger to face a single charge of carrying a needle. The new arrest put a bindle of crystal directly on him. Typically, California's Realignment law would block an addict like Roger from being sent to state prison. But Roger had a prior violent conviction for armed robbery in 1984, making him ineligible for "county prison." Nevertheless, a Calaveras judge allowed Roger to briefly escape the prison gates by entering program called Courage to Change.

For months Roger excelled in the setting, opening his own landscaping business, which employed six men and women who were on drug-related probation. Roger's muscular frame was returning, erasing the atrophy in his arms and the hollowed tightening on his ribs. The force came back into his singing voice. Slowly, a small host of treatment counselors and law enforcement officers began to believe in Roger Anderson again.

On a blistering summer morning Roger walked into Burson Full Gospel Church on the county's southwest border. He strolled by three wood crosses he had just built for the congregation, their scabrous, elegant shapes lifting against the cocoa-brown planks of the building prairie storefront, looking across the highway at a bleached 7-Up soda sign over an empty cinder block station, and casting long shadows down the gravel toward blond fields under the clouds.

During the church service Roger stood on a stage, urging the families to take a greater interest in helping local drug counselors and sheriff's deputies fight the human toll of methamphetamine.

"This is my rap sheet," he said, holding a stack of papers up high, his bicep creasing the sleeve of his western shirt. When

Roger's fingers half-opened, the linked sheets of paper fell scrolling down to the floor, where his left cowboy boot kicked the cascading records out even farther across the stage. A guffaw spurted through the audience. "This is me," Roger said. "This is what I was. And I'm not trying hide from it."

Roger had invited his former probation officer, Gino, to the church service. He now called Gino up to the stage. Roger handed Gino a certificate of law enforcement appreciation on behalf of the Burson Full Gospel Church community. Smiling to himself, he put his hand on Gino's shoulder, saying, "Hold on for a minute." Roger turned to the rows of expectant faces. "You know, Gino used to tell me that when people go out and get high, they put on their Superman capes again, because they want to be out there, flying at night." Roger reached over to a stool and grabbed a hidden red object. He squared up with Gino, face-to-face, man-to-man—and then unraveled a full Superman cape in front of him.

"Gino, I want you to know I'm officially turning my cape in to you," he said with a rough laugh, "because I don't want to be out there flying anymore."

The church members broke out in applause as the music came on and Roger took up a microphone, bringing his voice to bear on the hymn, "The Old Rugged Cross."

Looking on from the pews was his father, Martin. Burson's entire church congregation was celebrating that doctors had just declared Martin a victor in his bout with throat cancer. He was thin and quiet as he watched Roger electrifying the house of worshipers; but his eyes were awake over a faint, constant smile.

Also gazing on from the back was a 24-year-old recovering addict named Samantha. Roger had met her in the Courage to Change program. Roger, Samantha and everyone in the program had a "no relationships " clause in the official terms of their probation. She and Roger had received permission from the department for her accompanying him to church on Sundays, as well as a weekend trip to a Six Flags theme park. Both were wearing electronic ankle monitors. In June, probation agents used the devices to pinpoint a meeting between Roger and Samantha at the Black Bart Inn in San Andreas. At nearly the same time, Roger failed a drug test. He knew he was in trouble, though given the number of addicts he'd noticed slip up in Courage to Change by "pissing dirty," he thought the situation was manageable. He was wrong. Roger soon found himself in court on two counts of violating his probation. While in custody, Roger sent Samantha a letter and thus earned himself a third violation. Judge Douglas Mewhinney told Roger he'd had enough. The man called County was informed that his suspended state prison term for possession was being reinstated.

The first visit for Roger in county jail was from his parents, and it came with spiritually devastating news: Martin's throat cancer had returned. It was terminal.

"I'm in God's hands now, and so are you," Martin told his son. Thanks to a sympathetic jail commander, Martin and Mary were allowed two more visits with Roger before he was hauled away to Folsom Prison. Roger would always remember their final meeting. Martin had lifted himself up and slowly made his way to the door of the visitors' room. He paused, turned and looked over his shoulder at Roger. He mustered the strength to lift the hand holding his cane into a goodbye salute. And Roger knew it was the last time he would see his father.

The first day back at Folsom brought nothing fascinating to

Roger's eyes. In his younger days he'd mastered every nuance of prison culture. Now he had no interest in it. He avoided the power structure of the organized white inmate groups. He stayed away from anything that resembled smuggling or gang enterprise. Roger's only consolation was that during his last conversations with his father, it was clear that Martin believed, despite the recent slips, his son had truly left the essence of the drug world behind. It was a measure of faith and pride that no one that could take away. It was a belief that had to be realized. Roger was assigned a job as a welder and metal fabricator. He threw himself into community college courses offered in the prison, especially business management, business finance and business law. California inmates are allowed to keep up on current events if visitors bring them copies of newspapers. Roger did not dwell much on the headlines. He was too busy learning skills for his landscaping business, from marketing tactics and competitive strategies to the finer points of customer service.

For inmates around Roger who followed the news, there were plenty of crime-related stories and justice updates to keep up with, though California's Realignment law itself began to receive less media attention. The state was wilting under a recording breaking drought. Political parties were battling over education. A democratic assemblyman was arrested on federal corruption and gun-trafficking charges. For some reporters, Realignment was already a story of the past. One woman who refused to let the spotlight entirely vanish was Katie Tempesta. On a September afternoon Katie walked into a Fresno courthouse to once more face down her mother's killer. This time Michael Cockrell was not grinning from the defendant's box. After more than two years of negotiations between prosecutors and public defenders, Cockrell agreed to plead guilty to the premeditated murder of Lisa Gilvary, and the attempted murder of Lisa's roommate and police officer Jonathan Linzey. He also admitted to having a weapon inside the Fresno county jail immediately after the bloodshed. He was sentenced to forty years-to-life in prison.

The judge allowed Katie to make her victim's impact statement directly to Cockrell. With deep-drawn breaths echoing through the courtroom's microphone, Katie held her mother's ashes and recalled living with the horror Cockrell had unleashed. Lynne Brown sat at a close distance. She had been with Katie every step of the way. The two women left the courtroom together. "He really murdered himself," Katie told reporters on her way out.

While the ending of Katie's story was a rare example of newsprint California law enforcement officers were glad to read, it was clouded weeks later by an episode of shock for anyone wearing a badge. Almost one year to the day of the Sixth Street shoot out, in which gang member Sammy Duran engaged in a running firefight with Roseville police officers, another distressing call rang out over the same dispatch system. Roseville officers were told that an unknown suspect had just murdered Sacramento Sheriff's Deputy Danny Oliver over the county line before carjacking a citizen and shooting that victim in the head with a 9mm. The assailant, later identified as Luis Monroy, was speeding up Interstate 80 toward Roseville. Officers scrambled to find him. In the confusion that ensued, Monroy passed through Roseville and made it sixteen miles up the freeway to the city of Auburn, where he ambushed Placer County Sheriff's deputies with an AR-15 rifle. He wounded one deputy before assassinating a well-known homicide detective named Mike Davis Jr.

Similar to the gun battle with Duran, Monroy's standoff eventually ended when he was cornered in a house, surrounded by an army of cops and taken alive to face trial. The law enforcement community of Sacramento and Placer counties was stunned by the magnitude of destruction Monroy perpetrated in a matter of hours. For Roseville police detective Dave Buelow and the members of his narcotics team, the tragedy had an added element of surrealism: Monroy was a convicted drug dealer in multiple states with strong ties to Sinaloa, Mexico. He had twice been deported from the U.S. over drug and weapons charges. An unconfirmed report began circulating through area police departments that—like Sammy Duran the year before—Monroy was high on methamphetamine when he began shooting police officers; and while toxicology results are pending, the killer's history as a drug-runner is a matter of record.

Yet within days of massive funerals processions flashing through Roseville for Deputy Oliver and Detective Davis, California voters went to the polls and passed Proposition 47, which lowered possession of hardcore drugs to a simple misdemeanor, along with multiple property crimes. Realignment had already disconnected most drug convictions from the state prison system. Now, Prop. 47 had arguably relieved California's greater drug world from having to worry about the proverbial "rock bottom moment" even on the county level. Buelow was friends with Mike Davis, but beyond the mental bombshell of the officer-involved murders at the hands of a dealer was the question of how Buelow's team could do their jobs in the wake of Prop. 47. For three years he, Bret Brzyscz, Andy Palmore and their partners have investigated armed robberies, armed home invasions, serial burglaries, wide-scale identity theft rings and child endangerment cases all committed under the influence of methamphetamine or heroin.

In March, the team arrested a suspect named Travis Layton on charges of armed robbery and street terrorism. To their surprise Layton was out of custody within two months and allegedly threatening to kill a witness in the case against him. Buelow's investigators acted quickly, putting the cuffs on Layton for five felony counts of witness intimidation. At nearly the same time, the team encountered a meth addict named John Del Pozzo Jr., arresting him eight different times in the span of three weeks, on charges of burglary and identity theft. Placer County Jail records confirm that Del Pozzo was released seven times in three weeks without posting bail or having a judicial review. Each of Del Pozzo's seven arrests was for victimizing a different Roseville citizen through burglary, identity theft or the use of stolen credit cards. When a newspaper ran a story about Layton and Del Pozzo, Placer County Sheriff's officials acknowledged that pressures from California's Realignment law, coupled with a federal population cap on the jail, were forcing their staff to make tough decisions about which defendants awaiting trial get released. They also confirmed those discharges from custody were happening without bail attached and without judicial oversight.

Such realities were making it hard enough for Buelow and his partners to guard residents from crimes committed by addicts, but the passage of Prop. 47 amplified that stress tenfold. And in the last week before voters cast their ballots, the "victimless" talking points in favor of the law never mentioned the names Danny Oliver or Mike Davis Jr.

DRIVING OUT OF Sacramento County's fields and into the swaying, open pastures of Amador, Roger tries to come to terms with the present moment. His close friend James Livezey succumbed to brain cancer not long after being convicted of killing Marvin Brown in the Sequoia Rose Mobile Home Park. When Calaveras Sheriff's detectives Josh Crabtree and Wade Whitley captured Livezey at gunpoint along the dry, brushy banks of Lake Hogan, the fugitive told them he was not trying to run from judgment; but he knew he was dying, and he wanted to die with open sky over his head. In the end, Livezey spent his final days in an institutional coffin of stonewalls and steel bars.

But the gravesite forever on Roger's mind is that of his father: Martin Anderson passed away only months after Roger arrived at Folsom Prison. Roger penned a handful of letters to him. None arrived in time. Shortly before Martin expired, he woke up, delirious, and asked his wife and daughter, "Is Roger alright?"

Now, the cattle lands that his father loved so much come rolling through the windshield. Roger knows he can't take back what happened. He can only try to keep the last vows—spoken and unspoken—that he made to Martin. He can take care of his mother. He can lend a helping hand to neighbors in need. He can find a quiet dignity in hard work. In short, he can try to fill the empty cowboy boots his father's departure left in the community.

Roger has $500 in his pocket from the welding jobs he did in prison. Before the day is out, he has already been to the Calaveras office of the Department of Motor Vehicles to pay the registration on his work truck. Before the week is out he's lined up new landscaping jobs. Before the month is out he's already told one meth dealer to never call him again, while inviting several recovering addicts to his church.

"I just don't want to be involved in the madness anymore," he mutters, looking out on a radiant winter day in the foothills. "That story about me, while it's true, is in no way a reflection of my mother and father, who raised their other kids into adulthood as good, honest people. I went my own way, and made my own choices. So, for me, now it's about wanting to keep my promises, and trying to help other people look for a better way. In the end, it's just about being the man I need to be."

AUTHOR'S NOTE

SOME POTENTIAL CRITICISMS of this book are easy enough to see coming. It is simultaneously about jails, prisons, criminal thinking, addiction, mental illness and policy born from political exploitation, yet without staking out a hard, central focus on any one of them. Some readers will feel its investigative findings should have covered more than four states; or, conversely, will insist its stories should have been anchored in just one location. Still others may close this book with the feeling they have wandered through a disjointed anthology of dark factual narratives held together by the thinnest of threads, like some pearl necklace of real life despair, or maybe a house of mirrors where every turn flashes another ugly reflection that scarcely resembles the last one. For those who find the book's beacon disorienting, I can only say welcome to the daily experience of the criminal justice system. There are plenty of other books and articles that tug on a single coil of its Medusa head. In writing this, I wanted to offer a contextualized glimpse at the jagged mosaic that every cop, judge, attorney, victim's advocate and crime reporter is staring at, half-consciously, for the duration of what one might call a career.

Warren Ellis once said that if you're "miserable, edgy and tired," you're in the perfect mood for journalism." In my experience, the exhaustion that overcomes many investigative reporters is born from watching other members of press get away with timesaving maneuvers that undermine the public's belief in accurate and meaningful reportage. I have endeavored to take no shortcuts in these pages. This book is a work of journalism. The names of the law enforcement officers, attorneys, victims' advocates and experts are their real names. Similarly, criminals, addicts, drug dealers and suspects are identified by their true identities, as are witnesses to crimes who were the subject of testimony in open court.

In the case of the present-tense narratives, I was either physically present for the events chronicled, or had access to multiple people who were present and was able to speak to them within hours of the action taking place.

Any arrestee written about in this book was convicted in a court of law of crimes consistent with the events described, with the exception two cases that were still pending resolution. For more than fifteen months, Forrest Locke watched his charges for dealing heroin and assault and battery crawl through the Placer County court system in California. He had not been brought to trial when this book went to press. It is worth noting that I was with the narcotics detectives who arrested Locke on his heroin-dealing case, and I personally watched Locke call Derek Snider just minutes before police found the heroin in Snider's car, as well as the larger stash inside Locke's house. Cassandra Flor, a co-defendant in the same case, had also not been convicted at the time of publication. The case against Sammy Duran, who was charged with nine separate counts of attempted murder and one count of false imprisonment, had not even had a preliminary hearing, let alone a jury trial, at the time "The Cutting Four-piece" went into production. Duran was also prosecuted in Placer County. In Duran's case, I was present for much of the shoot-out and standoff, and was able to talk to numerous residents who knew Duran and spotted him through the course of the events described in Chapter 8. I was also able to view two different cell phone videos that were recorded in real-time as the drama unfolded, one of which eventually became an official piece of evidence in the case against Duran. In September of 2014, an independent report commissioned by Placer County supervisors found that the county's court system was "significantly" slow in handling felony cases.

Field research for this book began in January of 2012, the same month California's Realignment law began to go into full effect. Prior to that, between May of 2010 and October of 2011, I had spent eighteen months as an embedded reporter with rural county law enforcement agencies for the journalism book, "Shadow People: how meth-driven crime is eating at the heart of rural America." With a two-month break between fieldwork on that project and "The Cutting Four-piece," it is no exaggeration to say that for nearly five years I never left the so-called shadow people. However, with this investigation, I did engage them differently. My first project is told almost entirely from the point of view of patrol officers, detectives, prosecutors and victims' advocates. In this book, I have tried to balance those same perspectives with addicts, recovering addicts, inmates and ex-convicts. In addition to the names that appear in this book, I owe a special thanks to a number of people who I will not mention due to privacy concerns and a hope that their fortunes will turn in the days ahead.

Beyond the above parameters, two lynchpin interviews for this project were John Maki of the John Howard Association and Bryan Stevenson the Equal Justice Initiative. Maki granted me an extensive conversation by phone from his Chicago office on January 8, 2013. Additionally, the lengthy reports the JHA compiled on the Illinois prison system were of great help. On January 23, 2014 Bryan Stevenson granted me a graciously patient interview by phone from his office in Alabama. Prior to that, the speech Stevenson gave to the Illinois Judges Association on December 14, 2012 occurred at a critical juncture in my first year of research on this book. Several long interviews with Rosemary Collins, president of Alabama Citizens United for Rehabilitation of Errants, or Alabama CURE, were also of paramount help. Ms. Collins provided on the ground reports on Alabama's justice reform movement and reflections the life her own son lives everyday in prison.

There were subtle but meaningful differences between the working relationships I had with California law enforcement during the writing of "Shadow People" and the construction of this book. When I started "Shadow People," the command staffs of seven law enforcement agencies in five counties granted me varying levels of access to their patrol officers and investigators, knowing full well I was working on a national journalism project. When I started "The Cutting Four-piece," help came from familiar quarters. I told commanders at the Calaveras Sheriff's Department, the Amador Sheriff's Office and the Jackson Police Department— all of which had been highly involved in "Shadow People"—that I had a new enterprise on the complexities of probation, parole and recidivism levels. I was given casual clearance for more "ride-along" time, though in a much less scheduled and structured way than before. However, it was a particular law enforcement agency that was wholly new to me that would be critical to this book.

Five months into the project, I took over a newspaper crime desk at *The Roseville Press Tribune* in the north region of the greater Sacramento metropolitan. Going out to police incidents and living in Placer County courtrooms, I soon began doing ride-alongs with a few of Roseville's patrol officers and following a handful of the department's homicide, robbery and narcotics detectives. Clearance from the department came on an assignment-to-assignment basis, and was granted primarily for work related to my newspaper job. I never had a formal conversation with Roseville's command staff about this book. The gun battle that Roseville's officers were ensnared in with Sureño member Sammy Duran took place in a neighborhood three minutes from my newsroom, hence I was the first reporter to arrive on-scene, shortly after Agent Kenney had been shot but before most of the rounds had been exchanged. Unencumbered and unnoticed with a lack of cameras, microphones and news vans, I was able to blend in with the neighbors and watch most of the saga unfold from several vantage points. Either intentionally or unintentionally, I was not removed from the area and pushed back with the other reporters.

While the Rocklin and Citrus Heights police departments also donated valuable time to this journalism endeavor it is hard to measure the assistance that Roseville's officers eventually provided, especially in context of working for a city whose image is closely guarded and controlled by political consultants, business figures, bank officers and land developers.

In total, between seven law enforcement agencies, I spent some 210 hours following officers and detectives. I am in debt to a number of them whose names never appear in these pages, particularly Chris Crandell of the Amador County

District Attorney's Office, Jon Foosum of the Amador County Sheriff's Office, Jose Arevalos of the Jackson Police Department, Jeremy Garrison of the Citrus Heights Police Department, Ron Lawrence and Evan Adams of the Rocklin Police Department, and Vince Dutto, Dave Flood, Ryan Bal, Karl Dyer, Andrew Bonner, Darren Marks, Brian McGlincney and Jimmy Aguirre of the Roseville Police Department. Tom Shaer of the Illinois Department of Correction demonstrated an incredible amount of transparency in setting up my all-access tour of the Dixon Correction Center, for journalism that appeared first in my newspaper work and then later morphed into the entire narrative of chapter 9. Assistant Warden Gary Young of the Louisiana State Penitentiary in Angola offered as much access to his prison as any reporter could hope for, including allowing me to spend time behind the iron chutes with the inmate bull riders.

The author's note of "Shadow People" ended with mediation on the profound respect I developed for law enforcement officers while being embedded with them. I still hold that view. But the deepest personal insight from working on this project involves a profession different than police work—my own profession, or the tattered frays of what's left of it. This book would simply not have been possible without the tireless work and achievements of dozens of journalists around the United States. This includes national agencies such as *Reuters* and *Time Magazine*, to city newspapers, especially *The New Orleans Times-Picayune* and *The Palm Beach Post*, all the way to, and perhaps most vitally, community newspapers including *The Dixon Telegraph*, *Suak Valley Newspapers* and *The Calaveras Enterprise*. Without the work of such publications tackling the numbing, nebulous subject within these pages would have been an act of futility. This is book is intentionally built on a collective foundation of meaningful journalism. The reporters whose investigations and beat coverage were essential to the paths I ventured down are directly cited in the text. Additionally, the entire time I was assigned to cover California's Realignment experiment in Placer County my friend and colleague Raheem Hosseini was doing an excellent job reporting on it in neighboring Sacramento County for *The Sacramento News and Review*. His talent, commitment and willingness to constantly discuss his findings was a constant source of support.

I can hardly escape the haunting conclusion that a world without professional newspaper and magazine journalists would be a world in which my books, and countless more important books of the past and future, could never materialize. Even as I write these words next to a café window looking out on the Eisenhower Executive Building, a few hundred feet from the White House, I'm preparing for a somber meeting with journalists from around the nation. Among the faces waiting when I walk through the doors will be a correspondent who was abducted by Islamic fighters while working on the Syrian border, and another who had a portion of his face rebuilt after being shot along side U.S. troops in Afghanistan. When I hear that reporters with the level of expertise as these two gentlemen are struggling to find fair paying work it disturbs me. And it should disturb the reading public. In the same year that American journalists Jim Foley and Steven Sotloff were captured and beheaded in the Middle East, men like the correspondents I previously mentioned, who have more on-the-ground experience, are continuing their mission even as they struggle to make a livable wage. It speaks volumes to the fact that many of the journalists whose writing informed this project are likely wondering, possibly at this very moment, exactly how much longer they will be able to continue on in their jobs.

Leonard Pitts Jr. of *The Miami Herald* once said, "If newspapers die, crooks won't cry," a sentiment that was echoed by former *Baltimore Sun* reporter David Simon, who reflected, "Oh to be a state or local official in America without newspapers: It's got to be one of the great dreams in the history of American corruption." It is easy to blame advancing technology for the inability of so many reporters to keep providing accurate and objective findings for their communities. Too easy in fact, because the biggest threat to investigative work and institutional beat coverage is the belief that journalism is foremost a profit-seeking venture rather than a vital civic alarm system. In the nearly nine years I've been around the media landscape, I have seen countless newspaper groups attempt to cut their way to profitability by shedding talent and investigative output, to the point where their product became so superficial that few will ever be convinced to pay for it again.

Whether the reading public eventually decides to use its direct consumer voice to push back against the tide that's decimating journalism is something I cannot predict. But I do know the women and men whose reporting helped make this book possible—whose words on the page prevailed over financial stress, ongoing job insecurity and the knowledge that the "American dream" they document may be out of their own reach—have been heroic enough to the Republic in my eyes that I will always proud to have been associated with this profession, this crazed, irrational calling that makes us scribblers keep trying to endure.

—Scott Thomas Anderson
Washington D.C.
November, 2014